Whistleblowing: A Practical Guide

BRIAN MARTIN

Published 2013 by Irene Publishing Sparsnäs, Sweden
irene.publishing@gmail.com www.irenepublishing.com

This is a revised and updated version of *The Whistleblower's Handbook: How to Be an Effective Resister*, originally published in 1999 by Jon Carpenter in Charlbury, UK and Envirobook, Sydney.

© creative commons
Attribution-ShareAlike 3.0 Unported (CC BY-SA 3.0)

ISBN 978-1-291-54819-8

Layout and cover design: Tormod Otter Johansen

IRENE PUBLISHING RESISTANCE STUDIES SERIES

1. Tackling Trident, edited by Vinthagen, Kenrick & Mason
2. Beyond Celebrations - Analysing Impacts of the Nonviolent Arab Revolutions (forthcoming 2014), edited by Johansen
3. Whistleblowing: A Practical Guide by Martin
4. What would it take? How a strategy of unarmed resistance could win freedom in West Papua (forthcoming 2014) by MacLeod

Contents

Preface	5
1 Seven common traps	9
2 The problem	23
3 Speaking out and the consequences	29
4 Personal assessment: what should I do?	51
5 Preparation	65
6 Low-profile operations	81
7 Official channels	89
8 Leaking	129
9 Building support	151
10 Case studies: considering options	197
11 Surviving	229
12 Whistleblower groups	239
References	249

Quick reference guide

If you have a general interest in the topic,
start with chapter 1.

If you don't know what to expect if you speak out,
see chapter 3.

If you are trying to decide what to do about a situation,
see chapter 4.

If you are planning to do something,
see chapters 5 and 6.

If you are already involved in making a complaint,
see chapter 7.

If you're up against a deeply entrenched problem,
see chapters 8 and 9.

If you want to become active and work for social change,
see chapter 12.

Preface to the second edition

In 1998 and 1999, when I was writing the first edition of this book, I had been president of Whistleblowers Australia for several years, and regularly received phone calls from whistleblowers seeking advice and support. Their stories were remarkably similar, typically involving someone who spoke out about a problem at work, suffered reprisals and then tried to deal with the situation by going to some official channels such as ombudsmen but received no useful help. What I had to say in response was often along standard lines: identify your goals, analyse your situation, consider your options and take action — and don't rely on official channels.

Saying the same sort of thing over and over was becoming monotonous, so I decided to write a book spelling out what I knew in a clear and accessible fashion. At the time, there wasn't a whole lot of practical material for whistleblowers. The best advice manual was Tom Devine's *The Whistleblower's Survival Guide*, but it was oriented to the US situation, with half the text devoted to various US procedures and agencies.

Because whistleblowing follows a fairly predictable pattern, I set myself the task of writing a manual that could be read by anyone in the world who can read English. That meant it had to be general, rather than referring to specific legislation or circumstances. Therefore, I focussed on analysis, options and strategy, in an attempt to counter the common tendency to speak out first and then, encountering reprisals, assume that official agencies are the solution.

The book seems to have been useful to many readers. After the original print run sold out, I put the text on my website, making it freely available. I was happy to leave it that way, until my friend Jørgen Johansen suggested I prepare a second edition. He had heard how useful the book was to a Norwegian whistleblower. Having set up a new publishing operation, Jørgen wanted to make the book available again in print.

As I worked on this second edition, I found much of the general advice to be just as relevant as it was years ago. But times have changed, especially with the impact of the Internet, and I found more to change than I had expected. The arrival of WikiLeaks on the scene has publicised an option — leaking — that already existed but had not been considered very often by whistleblowers. So I have added a new chapter about leaking, the challenge being to write it in a general way that won't be dated in a year or two because of new technological developments in communication and surveillance. I've also added a chapter on low-profile operations, an approach that deserves far more attention.

In the past couple of decades, whistleblowing has received ever more attention, especially in the media. In the early 1990s, the very term "whistleblower" was somewhat disreputable. Today, the label is more commonly worn with pride. There is a lot more whistleblower legislation, but little evidence that it provides all that much protection. The big change is the huge amount of information available on the Internet. Instead of whistleblowers ringing to obtain information and advice, they now search the web to learn on their own. I am far more likely to receive requests via email than by telephone.

Although there is plenty of information, only some is helpful in a practical way, especially in helping to think strategically. Therefore, I think there is a continuing role for this book.

For the first edition, I sent the text to several highly experienced individuals who regularly gave advice to whistleblowers. Three of them — Jean Lennane, Isla MacGregor and Lesley Pinson — wrote comments that I incorporated into the text. This time around, I have followed the same process, so now you will also find comments from two other experienced whistleblower advisers, Robina Cosser and Cynthia Kardell. Each of these individuals also provided suggestions that helped improve the text, as did Gabriele Bammer, AJ Brown, Stewart Dean, Margaret Love, Ted Mitew and one person who prefers to remain anonymous.

One of the most promising developments in recent years has been the gradually increasing number of experienced whistleblower advisers, in several countries. This manual can at most give a general approach to options. For more personalised advice, it is worthwhile tracking down knowledgeable individuals in your country and area of interest.

1 Seven common traps

> People seeking to expose wrongdoing often fall into seven common traps.
>
> - Trusting too much
> - Not having enough evidence
> - Using the wrong style
> - Not waiting for the right opportunity
> - Not building support
> - Playing the opponent's game
> - Not knowing when to stop

Society desperately needs principled and courageous people, and it needs them to be effective in exposing problems and promoting solutions. You can call them workers and citizens who are doing their ethical duty or you can call them whistleblowers, dissidents, agitators, conscientious objectors or whatever. The name doesn't matter much, but effectiveness does.

Unfortunately, many of the principled and courageous people who set out to expose wrongdoing are completely unsuccessful. They fall into standard traps. This is partly because they are trusting. They trust people in power and they believe what they've been taught about how the system operates. Their cynical co-workers wouldn't try anything so foolish.

This is not a book about ethics. It is about people who act on the basis of principles such as honesty, accountability and human welfare and who resist corruption, discrimination and exploitation. It's not about people who "resist" primarily to serve their own interests.

1. Trusting too much

There's a serious problem: money is being siphoned from accounts; the organisation's public statements are misleading; cronies without skills are being promoted. What to do? An honest, community-spirited person of course reports the problem. Naturally managers will be eager to fix the problem — or will they?

For those who discover problems, one of the biggest traps is to trust that others will also be concerned and take action. Many whistleblowers, burned by their experiences, say that they were naive. They trusted. They trusted that management would act. They trusted that co-workers would support them. They trusted that the union would back them. They trusted that government agencies and the courts would work to ensure justice. They trusted that others would do the right thing and hence didn't expect retaliation. They didn't anticipate that their efforts might fail.

Sometimes this trust is warranted, but all too often it is not. Cynical workers don't act because they assume management knows about and tolerates the problem and that if they do anything about it they will suffer reprisals. In many cases they are right.

Helen was a conscientious employee in a large employment agency. After being promoted into a new position, she began to notice a bias in results. Some clients had only a small chance of success, whereas others — who paid a "bonus fee" — received favoured treatment. She talked about it with her boss, who explained that the fee and other gratuities were a standard part of the business. She became even more disturbed and wrote a memo to the chief executive officer asking for a review of the bonus fee system. Within a few days she was carpeted by her boss for inadequate performance, especially for alleged complaints received from clients a year earlier. She then raised the issue of bonus fees at a staff meeting. None of her colleagues would support her. She gradually realised that the bonus fee was part of a system of bribery accepted by all managers. After being fired, Helen sued her former employer on the grounds of unfair dismissal. Her professional association refused to support her. In the middle of the hearing, it became apparent that her lawyer had been conspiring with the company.

Helen had stumbled upon a corrupt practice that was so entrenched that everyone accepted it as the way things were done. She trusted her boss; she trusted her CEO; she trusted her co-workers; she trusted her professional association and her lawyer. Could she trust anyone at all?

2. Not having enough evidence

Humans have a great capacity to think up explanations for things they observe. However, because more than one explanation might be possible, it's important to obtain additional evidence to confirm or deny what you think is happening.

This is just what detectives are supposed to do when investigating crimes. It is also what a concerned worker or citizen needs to do when discovering something suspicious.

The big trap here is to make claims about what's going on without first having evidence to back up every detail. The claims might be

The examples

The examples in this handbook are not directly based on actual cases, in whole or part. They do draw on common themes in real cases, and are intended to illustrate points that become familiar to anyone who listens to dozens of stories. The examples differ in a few ways from actual cases.

- Most actual cases are incredibly complex, with all sorts of details and byways. It's impossible to convey such complexity in a paragraph or two.
- Actual cases are far more traumatic for the target of the attack than any description can suggest. (See chapter 11 for more on this.)
- In actual cases there are real people and real consequences. Without knowing the people involved it is hard to grasp the personal dimensions.
- The attacks I describe are bad enough, but in many actual cases the attacks are far worse: spiteful, insidious, unremitting and intensely debilitating. If anyone thinks the examples here are unrealistic, they're right: the reality could be even grimmer.

For those who'd like to read about actual cases, there are many good references given at the end of the book. Even better is to talk to someone who has been there.

entirely correct, but claims without evidence can be plausibly denied, and even ones with evidence can be discredited. Furthermore, the evidence needs to be solid, so the facts make the case without the addition of suspicion or speculation

Fred was a customs officer who had just moved to a new posting. He began to notice that certain types of goods were always put through on a particular shift involving the same group of officers. He knew from previous experience that these types of goods were regularly used to smuggle drugs. In the face of much resistance, he managed to get on the shift himself, and uncovered a major drugs shipment. Then he was transferred to a less desirable job. He went to the media with claims of corruption in customs. But in the face of bland denials by customs officials, nothing could be done. There wasn't enough hard evidence even to justify an inquiry.

Fred was stymied in his career in customs, so he obtained a job in a trucking company checking inventories. With his nose for corruption, he soon detected a scam in which certain goods were trucked without going through accounts, in return for a bribe. This time Fred collected detailed evidence, including taped conversations and photos. But he wrecked his credibility by claiming that the operation was approved by top management. This was probably true but, without hard proof, regulators could do nothing. Fred lost his job. He won his case for unfair dismissal but the managers sued him for defamation, successfully shifting the focus from their culpability to Fred's behaviour.

3. Using the wrong style

Who is more believable: a serious-looking and sober-sounding scientist or a dishevelled, ranting street-corner speaker? As much as we might disapprove, style is a crucial part of getting a message across.

People who try to expose problems such as child abuse, public health risks and corruption are usually outraged. Yet an approach with too much overt emotion — shouting, hectoring, disgust — can be counterproductive. A sensible, to-the-point approach may be more effective.

It is possible, though rare, to appear to be too calm. An effective style hits the right note for a relevant audience.

Another problem is that concerned people get enormously involved in the issue. They are so involved that they forget that others know little or nothing about it. They jump right into the middle of the story without explaining the background.

Allen was the victim of a construction swindle. He had contracted for improvements to his home. After paying $100,000, the work done was woefully inadequate, and a different contractor quoted Allen $100,000 to fix the problems. However, the original contractor claimed that Allen owed him money and refused to do anything until being paid. The building industry watchdog body took a year to decide there was no case to answer. Allen berated anyone who couldn't get away. Even sympathisers soon became tired of his tirades. He compiled a 45-page document titled "BUILDING INDUSTRY CORRUPTION." It was filled with statements of outrage and extreme claims, including letters he had written to various official bodies. He sent this document to hundreds of politicians and government departments, but only received a few polite letters in response. Even though he had a good case, Allen's style screamed "crank."

4. Not waiting for the right opportunity

Many a good exposé is ineffective because it is made at the wrong time, to the wrong audience or in the wrong circumstances. Many people believe that the truth is enough on its own and that it shouldn't matter when or how they speak out. But it does! Even after carefully collecting evidence, it may be necessary to wait months or even years to have the best chance of making a difference. It's a common trap for people with an important message to go public as soon as they are ready — rather than when the opportunity is just right.

Dolores, an experienced political activist, collected evidence of surreptitious donations to a political party from foreign vested interests. She made contact with an investigative journalist, who produced a series of excellent stories in a major newspaper. However, the party was able to weather the storm without much difficulty — it had just been elected to office with a large majority and was enjoying a honeymoon period with the public and media. No other outlets took up the story. Just over a year later, though, the party's popularity had dropped, it was in the midst of a bitter internal fight and an opposition party was sniffing for blood. The same story would have been dynamite at the time, but since it had already been broken, journalists were not as interested as they might have been.

5. Not building support

If truth was enough by itself, it shouldn't be necessary to build support. It would simply be enough to speak the truth. Relying solely on the truth is a serious trap. To have some chance of success, it is vital to have supporters. This often requires a patient effort to find out where people stand and then to mobilise those who are sympathetic, win over some of those who are neutral and to reduce the hostility of some of the opponents. It's not enough to be correct and to be serving the public interest.

When the old-fashioned politician — without money for media campaigns — goes door-to-door meeting people and exchanging ideas and plans, this is a form of grassroots politics. A similar process is required in organisations and communities on many issues, even when the facts are clear-cut. It is tempting to skip this laborious process and just run with the facts. It's often disastrous.

Frank was a social worker with lots of experience. Tired of the big-city rat-race, he moved to a small town, where he was attached to the local hospital. Soon after arriving, he started receiving reports of abusive behaviour by a local government official, Peterson, including verbal abuse and assault of Peterson's neighbours and anyone who dared criticise him. Frank arranged a private meeting with the mayor. He described some of what he'd heard, suggested some constructive responses and asked for advice. Not long after, he was dismissed from the hospital. Six people — five clients and one person he'd never met — filed complaints about him, including sexual assault. These complaints were written up in the local newspaper. Frank was referred to a psychiatrist and had his licence as a social worker removed. He only found out later that Peterson had lots of connections in the town, including a brother who was the hospital superintendent and a nephew who was editor of the paper.

6. Playing the opponent's game

There are all sorts of agencies and formal processes for dealing with injustices, including grievance procedures, ombudsmen, antidiscrimination boards and the courts. When an individual appeals to one of these agencies for action to be taken against abuses in an organisation, the organisation's managers have all the advantages: far more money, unlimited time and usually little individual responsibility. Managers can stall, resist giving information, hire expensive lawyers and mount attacks.

In many cases, to stick to formal channels is to play the opponent's game largely by the opponent's rules. The individual is worn

Jeffrey Wigand was a tobacco company whistleblower. He was played by Russell Crowe in the film The Insider.

down emotionally and financially while the organisation continues on, unchecked and unchanged. Even if the individual wins a settlement, it is usually years down the track, is too little and too late for much satisfaction, and does nothing to change the original problem.

Agencies and formal processes present themselves as means to justice, and many people believe in them. They trust the system to provide a means of policing itself — an extension of trap #1, trusting too much.

If you're going to use formal processes, you had better learn the rules well. When playing the opponent's game, the rules might actually be used against you.

Joy received a faulty diagnosis from an established physician and was treated incorrectly for two years, leading to additional health problems and costing her tens of thousands of dollars in lost income and expenses, not to mention pain and suffering. She had kept meticulous documentation and obtained correct diagnoses from several doctors. One of them confidentially told her that she was only one of many who had been misdiagnosed by this physician. Joy made a complaint to the medical appeals tribunal. After a desultory investigation and 18 months, it reported that no action would be taken. She followed up with a complaint to a consumer justice board. This time the process took over two years, with a similar result. Finally, she sued the physician for damages. The physician's insurance company delayed the case for three years and then mounted a smear operation, questioning her motives and sanity. Joy finally won the case after five years. The insurance company appealed and, several years later, eventually won the appeal. Meanwhile, the physician retired with his public reputation untarnished.

7. Not knowing when to stop

Once embarked on a quest for justice, it can be hard to let go and get on with life. This is related to the type of psychological phenomenon by which people, after losing money, are inclined to risk more to recoup the loss. Yet often it's better to cut your losses and go on to more productive activities. This is especially true when it's apparent that the chance of success is small or that further gains will require more effort for far less return.

It's useful to remember that your family and friends didn't decide to take a risk: you did. You need to take their needs into account throughout your journey.

Some of those who have a commitment to justice and truth become used to hearing others say they are wasting their time. If they had listened to every sceptic they would have never acted in the first place. But the real trade-off is not between action and no action, but rather between different types of action. When the use-by date of a campaign arrives, it's time to shift to a different diet, otherwise the taste will become ever more bitter.

Helena was a high school art teacher who had taught for many years at different schools, moving because of her husband's career. She liked to experiment with different teaching methods and was popular with students and other teachers. At one school, though, the young authoritarian principal was threatened by her success and popularity. He arranged to get her fired after a series of negative evaluations and trumped up charges. Deeply shocked, she tried several formal channels and after five years received a substantial pay-out, though the details remained confidential and no action was taken against the principal. Helena wouldn't let go of the case, though, and continued to write letters to politicians and government agencies and to tell the story to anyone who would listen. She did not return to teaching or take any other job.

Conclusion

People shouldn't be blamed for falling into these traps. Even those with years of experience in difficult jobs are like babes in the woods when suddenly confronted with the full force of the system. Why wouldn't they trust people with whom they had worked for years? Where would they have learned skills in collecting and sticking to evidence, developing an effective style and waiting for the right moment? How would they have learned organising skills when it's not part of the job? How would they know that formal processes give only an illusion of justice when everyone assumes that they are there to fix problems? After years in a lonely struggle and many betrayals, how are they to make a sensible judgement about the next step — and when to bow out?

No, falling into these traps is entirely predictable, which is why story after story sounds much the same. It is only by learning from what happens to others, and from the accumulated wisdom of dissidents and justice-seekers, that a better path forward can be navigated. The following chapters give some idea of what's involved.

Frank Serpico, a New York police officer, exposed police corruption. In the 1973 film Serpico, *he was played by Al Pacino.*

2 The problem

> Figure out what the problem is and what causes it.

The problem is that something is seriously wrong and no one is able or willing to do anything about it. Here are some examples.

- A company is regularly defrauding clients by adding a fee for an unnecessary (and unperformed) service.
- Many employees receive confidential payments — bribes — in order to ignore a violation of procedure.
- Friends of a particular boss are given jobs, promotions and special opportunities; those who have fallen out of favour with this boss are given a hard time.
- In applying policy, certain groups are discriminated against: an ethnic minority, members of a certain religion, backers of a particular political party.
- An organisation persists in a practice that is hazardous to the public.
- A boss humiliates subordinates, causing many to resign or take sick leave due to stress.

- Blatant sexual harassment by one particular powerful individual is tolerated by top management.
- The public relations department is instructed to lie to the public to cover up a serious mistake by managers.
- The high ideals of an organisation are ignored by most employees, who find it safer to do shoddy work.
- A manager is embezzling money.

The central issue is how to solve the problem. But first, a preliminary question. Do you want to try to help solve the problem? Perhaps you don't care. Perhaps you have been part of the problem, and don't plan to change. If so, this book is not for you. If you do care, then this book *is* for you.

If you want to try to help fix the problem, then the central issue is how. What is the first step? Who will be willing to help? What are the likely repercussions? Is it possible to make a difference? Is it worth doing anything? When there are several problems, which should be the first priority? These questions are dealt with in later chapters.

Let's look a bit more at the problems. They involve all sorts of different areas. But many of them fit a few categories.

- Injustice, unfairness and discrimination. This includes bias in favour of friends or relatives and bias against out-groups.
- Violations of laws and/or morality. This includes stealing, bribery and deception.
- Dangerous practices. This includes causing hazards to health and the environment.
- Abusive behaviour. This includes bullying, harassment and scapegoating.
- Complicity. This is covering up or doing nothing about a problem.

Is it bribery?

It is important to work out exactly what you think the problem is, and why you think it's a problem.

Example A pharmaceutical company has been selling a certain drug for several years. Some of the company's scientists came up with a finding that suggests a new risk for certain users. It has been a year since the scientists reported on their finding but the drug is still being sold the same way, with no change in the information sheet about adverse effects.

What is the problem? One problem is a potential danger to the public. Another is that the drug's information sheet is incomplete: this might be considered false advertising or, in other words, lying. Finally, there may be complicity: the unwelcome data are being knowingly ignored. On the other hand, management may say there's no problem at all, since the new finding has not been confirmed and they don't want to alarm people who are benefiting from the drug.

Which problem is most important to tackle? Is it to alert consumers to the hazard? Is it to undertake more research to gain a better understanding of the risk? Is it to change the company's approach to possible drug risks, so that consumer safety is given a higher priority? Is it to change the culture of conformity, in which no one wants to do anything that might harm sales of a profitable drug? Of course, you might be concerned about all these problems. But to be effective, it's useful to know where your priorities lie.

The source of problems

It can be very helpful to understand why a problem arises and why it persists. The most immediate explanation is that a person or group has something to gain, typically money, power or status. Financial fraud can be motivated by greed. Hazardous practices can be motivated by the push for profits. Claiming credit for other people's ideas can be motivated by the desire for promotion. Covering up for mistakes by colleagues can be motivated by the desire to protect the group's reputation for good work. To begin an analysis of the source of a problem, ask "who has something to gain?"

Although many problems can be explained this way, there are numerous exceptions. Sometimes the immediate explanation doesn't work. A company might be losing millions of dollars due to fraud but managers don't do anything about it. This might be because the managers are in on the fraud. Another possibility is that if anyone tried to stop the fraud, they would get no support or even come under attack, so it's just easier to let it continue.

Cynthia Kardell comments

If a problem could be caused by either corruption or incompetence, it is more likely to be incompetence. So, in getting someone to investigate, it's best to call it incompetence and let the investigator discover whether it is corruption. Making an exaggerated claim might persuade the investigator that you should not be taken seriously.

Another sort of explanation is that problems occur because of the way things are organised. Instead of blaming individuals, this explanation traces problems to procedures, organisational structures and sets of expectations. For example, the rules on safety at a workplace might be so complicated and difficult to follow that most workers ignore them just to get the job done. It is easy to blame the workers for not following the rules or management for not enforcing them, but perhaps a better approach is to simplify and clarify the rules.

In the case of burglary, many blame the burglars. Others blame parents for not bringing up children to be honest, or teachers for not educating students properly. But does blame help solve the problem? Another approach is to look at solutions that involve changing the system. Perhaps if there were more opportunities for satisfying work, fewer people would resort to burglary. Perhaps part of the problem is the pervasive role of advertising and commercialism, which present acquisition of products as the symbols of success, and make some people feel excluded. These are explanations that blame "the system" or "society" rather than individuals. You don't need to agree with any particular explanation in order to realise there is a difference between blaming individuals and seeing the problem as due to procedures or structures.

Psychologists have found it is very common for people to blame individuals for problems rather than social arrangements. For example, if the government develops a bad policy, it is easy and common for critics to blame politicians, often a particular politician. It is harder to grasp and adopt a less individualistic explanation, for example that there is a complex interaction between pressure groups, legislative restrictions and media-driven expectations that led to the policy in spite of everyone's good intentions.

The explanation does make a difference. If problems are seen as due to individuals, then the solution is usually to deal with the individuals, for example to replace or discipline them. Sometimes this works but often the problem continues on as before. If the organisational structure gives ample opportunities for fraud, then it's not much use getting rid of a few individuals, since their replacements are likely to succumb sooner or later. A better approach would be to change the structure. But that's usually a much more difficult task.

3   Speaking out and the consequences

If you speak out, you may be attacked.

- There are many methods of attack.
- To reduce outrage over their actions, attackers regularly use the methods of cover-up, devaluation, reinterpretation, official channels, intimidation and rewards.
- There are several reasons for attack.
- You should determine who is causing the problem.
- The attackers feel entirely justified — you should understand the way they think.

Occasionally those who speak out about problems are treated with the respect and seriousness they deserve. After all, if everyone tolerates corruption and dangerous practices, the problems will continue. The person who speaks out is the key to finding a solution. Sometimes — just sometimes — that's actually what happens. When an actual fire is threatening lives, the person who yells "fire!" is applauded.

If only it was always that easy! In lots of cases, unfortunately, the warning is treated entirely differently. It is a signal to attack the person who gave the warning.

Fred was a building surveyor. He noticed that a block of houses, a decade old, was built on unstable soil in an area potentially vulnerable to slippage. He made a routine report about this; nothing was done. Fearing the consequences of a major storm, he made his concerns known to the builder and the relevant local authorities. In the following months he noticed he was being shunned by some of his colleagues. He noticed his commissions were dropping off. Then there was a formal complaint about his performance. (And so on.)

Mary was a new surgeon in a hospital, working under a prominent doctor in the field. She noticed that he was making poor judgements in some cases and that he had been using a lot of drugs, easily obtained at the hospital. After she made a cautious comment to him about it, he began to criticise her performance at every opportunity, as his own continued to deteriorate. Then she reported her concerns to the hospital administrator. The next time one of her patients did poorly, she was carpeted, reprimanded and put on notice for dismissal. (And so on.)

Arnie was a young policeman, intelligent and enthusiastic. He discovered that many of his colleagues, on getting to the scene of a burglary, would steal things themselves before the owners arrived. Since he refused to participate himself, his colleagues became suspicious or hostile. Then he reported his observations to a police integrity unit. Although the unit was supposed to keep all such reports confidential, shortly afterwards Arnie was openly abused by his colleagues, being called a "dog" and other names. He was repeatedly reprimanded for slight or imaginary violations of dress code and driving. His wife received threatening phone calls. (And so on.)

Jacki, who lived near a light industrial district, found out about plans for a new plant that would produce a chemical she had heard about. After talking to some friends and local experts, she learned that the chemical production process could cause a long-term environmental hazard and that similar plants had been opposed in other localities. She held a meeting with neighbours, wrote a letter to the newspaper and organised a petition. She then found out that slanderous rumours were being spread about her motives and mental health. The police searched her house for drugs, supposedly on the basis of an anonymous tip. She was served with a writ for defaming the chemical company. Her children were harassed at school. (And so on.)

Methods of attack

Many techniques are used against those who speak out. Some of them are:

- Ostracism
- Harassment
- Spreading of rumours
- Threats (of reprimands, dismissal, etc.)
- Referrals to psychiatrists
- Censorship of writing
- Blocking of appointments
- Blocking of promotions
- Withdrawal of financial support
- Forced job transfers
- Being given impossible tasks
- Denial of work opportunities
- Formal reprimands
- Legal actions
- Dismissal
- Blacklisting
- Putting in danger
- Stalking
- Physical assault

The most common reprisal for speaking out is *ostracism*. This is when co-workers turn away rather than saying hello, when they sit at another table during tea breaks and lunch, when they stop dropping by to have a chat, and when they make excuses to leave whenever you approach them. Co-workers might be afraid to talk to you because bosses have warned them not to. Friendly or at least cordial relations with co-workers are highly important for job satisfaction. Hence this "cold shoulder" treatment can be very hard to handle. Another common reprisal is *harassment*. This can be quite petty. For example:

- You no longer get helpful hints on upcoming jobs.

- You are given no notice of meetings.
- You are given less desirable tasks.
- You are asked to carry out unnecessary bureaucratic procedures that are normally ignored or postponed, and then to repeat them due to minor discrepancies.
- The company car is never ready when you need it (but it is for others).
- Your requests for leave are misplaced or approved only for inconvenient times.
- Your roster ends up being unnecessarily awkward.
- You are asked to change offices several times.
- Your normal job, at which you are skilled, is given to someone else.
- You are given too much work.
- You aren't given enough work.

Rumours are common enough in any organisation or neighbourhood. As a form of reprisal, they can be especially vicious, and also attack a person's reputation in a pointed fashion.

Robina Cosser comments

Bosses sometimes tell people there is a *secret reason* why you have to be punished — and that they will get into serious trouble if they discuss the situation. This tactic can turn your supporters into helpless bystanders.

A common way to discredit someone is to say they are mentally ill. This is more pointed when they are formally required to see a psychiatrist. This is a form of harassment and can also fan the rumour mill.

Reprimands, censorship, blocking of appointments and promotions, withdrawal of financial support, forced job transfers, legal actions and dismissal — all these are straightforward forms of attack. Reprimands, legal actions and dismissal are obvious enough: if your boss serves you with a writ for defamation, you can be in no doubt about who is the target. On the other hand, it is usually hard to know why your application for a job has failed, unless you have inside information.

There's one extra level to all these forms of reprisal: the *threat* that they might be applied. You might be told you'd better be careful in order to avoid a formal reprimand. Comments might be made that those who criticise the organisation's policies will have a difficult time getting promoted. You might be threatened with a transfer, a legal action or dismissal.

Blacklisting is when many different employers in a field conspire not to employ someone. If you've exposed corruption in your firm and are dismissed, it can be difficult enough to get a job elsewhere. If other firms find out about the dismissal, perhaps due to a few quiet words, you may be denied employment in the field altogether.

Finally, there can be threats and attacks on your physical safety. For example, the wheel nuts on your car might be loosened, leading to a potentially hazardous breakdown at high speeds. Assaults and creation of hazards are a reality in many workplaces, and there are even murders. However, physical violence is used in only a small fraction of reprisals. One reason is that violence can backfire, creating sympathy for the victim, because physical attack is difficult to justify. In contrast, ostracism and petty harassment are more subtle and harder to expose.

Robina Cosser, vice president of Whistleblowers Australia.
(Sharan Rai Photography www.sharanrai.com)

What powerful attackers do

Powerful individuals and groups — called powerholders here — include governments, corporations, police and senior officials in organisations. When they do something potentially seen as unfair or wrong — anything from harassment to torture — they often take action to reduce adverse reactions, namely to prevent or decrease feelings of concern, anger, disgust or outrage. Five types of methods are regularly used.

1. Cover-up. The unfair actions are hidden from wider audiences, for example through secrecy or censorship.
2. Devaluation of the target. Anyone who threatens the powerholders, for example by exposing their actions, is discredited through rumours, circulation of damaging information, denunciations and referral to psychiatrists, among other methods.
3. Reinterpretation of the action. The events are explained in a way favourable to the powerholders, using lies, minimising of consequences, blaming others and presenting things from the perspective of the powerholders. For example, unfair dismissal might be explained as due to a funding cut or reorganisation.
4. Official channels that give the appearance of justice. Official channels such as courts and grievance procedures offer the promise of justice, but seldom deliver when powerholders are responsible for problems. See chapter 7 for more on this.
5. Intimidation and rewards. Targets and their allies may be threatened and subjected to reprisals. Attractive opportunities — jobs, promotions, protection, pay-offs — may be offered to those willing to support the attackers.

If top managers are involved in corruption, it is predictable that they will use cover-up, devaluation, reinterpretation, official channels and/or intimidation/rewards to reduce awareness and action against their corrupt behaviour. When they take reprisals against whistleblowers, they often use the very same methods to reduce outrage about the reprisals.

Be prepared for these methods. To counter them, you can use counter-methods.

1. Expose the problem. This is the counter to cover-up. It is why speaking out is so powerful.
2. Validate the target. You need to show you are credible and be able to maintain your credibility in the face of attempts at devaluation. See chapter 5.
3. Interpret the action as an injustice. You need to emphasise the injustice and to counter the lies, minimising, blaming and framing tactics used by the other side.
4. Build support. Instead of relying on official channels, you should seek to win allies and mobilise supporters to take action. See chapter 9.
5. Resist intimidation and rewards. To tackle the problem, you — or someone — need to be able to stand up to intimidation and refuse rewards.

You don't have to do all this on your own. You can work with others. See chapter 9. The key point here is to think about what the perpetrators are likely to do, and plan accordingly.

Reasons for attack

You've spoken out and then come under attack. That means that you've come under attack because you've spoken out. Right? Well, yes in many cases. But not always. A person can come under attack for all sorts of reasons. Here are some of them.

Bad luck. You are blamed for something just because you were in the wrong place at the wrong time.

Mistake. Your name was mentioned only because someone was confused.

Personal dislike. Someone — maybe your boss — doesn't like you. Maybe you remind them of a parent or spouse. Maybe you have a mannerism that annoys someone. You are victimised.

Scapegoating. Bad practices have been in place for a long time and have just been exposed. It's convenient to blame someone. You are a convenient target.

Caught in the crossfire. There's a long-standing feud between two powerful factions. Anyone and anything is used to wage the struggle. You are attacked as a means to get at someone else.

Obstinacy. Some bosses, after they begin a course of action, will proceed no matter what. Whatever the reason for coming under scrutiny to begin with — bad luck, a mistake, etc. — you are now a perpetual target. In this way, the boss's original judgement is vindicated.

The first step is to decide whether you're under attack. If so, the next step is to decide why you're under attack. The next question after that is what to do about it. That's the subject of the next chapter.

Most people prefer not to be attacked at all. Of course not! Many of those who speak out don't expect any reprisals. They see a problem and report it, assuming that all reasonably minded people will then investigate and do something to fix it.

When people know reprisals are possible, that changes things. People become afraid and most of them don't speak out. The problems fester.

Who is causing the problem?

In many disputes, both sides believe they are the victim. Rachel raised concerns about record-keeping and suffered all sorts of false accusations and abuse. But Rachel's boss and co-workers believe it is Rachel who has made false accusations and abused them. Who is right?

There's no absolute way to know, especially for those in the middle of the dispute. In many cases, the accounts from the two sides are so different that an outsider wouldn't know they are talking about the same situation.

Ultimately, the only way to determine the source of the problem is to carry out a detailed investigation, obtaining as many facts as possible. A judgement about the facts must be based on a set of values, such as common community assessments of what is honest and proper.

Even without a full investigation, there are some good pointers you can use as guides to what is probably going on.

- The double standard test.
- Timing.
- Who has the power?
- Who are complaints made to?
- Who is willing to discuss the issues?

The double standard test. Is one person being treated differently from another? If so, there is a double standard. Commonly, there is one standard for ordinary employees and another — much more demanding — for employees who question or challenge those in power.

Rachel is given a reprimand for being half an hour late three times in a month, while co-workers are later more frequently. That appears to be a double standard: Rachel is being singled out for criticism.

The double standard test is extremely useful in determining whether someone has been victimised for speaking out or otherwise challenging the system. Double standards are also to be expected in forms of systematic discrimination, such as bias against women, ethnic minorities or lesbians and gays.

Timing. If a person speaks out and then suddenly is subjected to criticism or harassment — allegedly on other grounds — this should give a strong suspicion that the criticism and harassment are a consequence of speaking out.

Rachel had been doing her job for years and always received favourable performance reviews. Immediately after she raised concerns about record-keeping, the boss and other senior people suddenly found a lot to criticise about her performance. They alleged that she had missed meetings, been abrasive, filled out forms incorrectly, been a poor performer, etc. Some complaints about her from a disgruntled customer were pulled out of a file, even though they had been made five years previously and never shown to Rachel. Things that were dismissed as trivial previously were blown up into major issues.

The key thing is that criticisms weren't made before the person spoke out, but were made afterwards. A close look at timing reveals a lot about who is causing the problem.

Who has the power? If one side or person has more power than another, it is possible to use that power to suppress dissent. Rachel may receive a reprimand from her boss, but she can't give a formal reprimand to her boss. There's an intrinsic asymmetry in any hierarchy.

Just because one side has more power doesn't mean that the other side is in the right. Rachel might have all her facts wrong and be causing distress among her co-workers by her behaviour.

If there are allegations by both sides that the other side is suppressing free speech, it is worth looking at who (if anyone) has the power to stop someone's speech. Those who don't have much power can't do much to suppress others.

Who are complaints made to? In a dispute or disagreement between fair-minded people, there is open discussion of the issues without threats or exercise of power against the other side. In a case of suppression of dissent, one side attempts to use power to silence the other.

The fairest way to make a complaint is directly to the person complained about. That way they know what the complaint is and have an opportunity to respond and perhaps to fix the problem. In contrast, a complaint to a person's boss is often an unfair method, especially if the person complained about doesn't receive a copy or even know about the complaint.

Jason has been blogging about the health hazards of eating meat. Many of his blogs are reproduced and recommended by others.

Response A. Helen, an independent meat advocate, writes her own blog rebutting Jason's claims.
Response B. A representative of the Beef Industry Forum responds to Jason's blogs, rebutting his claims.
Response C. Helen writes Jason a vehement letter criticising his views.
Response D. The Beef Industry Forum sends Jason documents presenting its viewpoint.
Response E. Helen sends a letter of complaint to Jason's boss.
Response F. The head of the Beef Industry Forum rings Jason's boss to complain.

Response G. The Beef Industry Forum compiles and sends a dossier about Jason and his alleged personal shortcomings and sends it to the website administrator hosting his blog, but not a copy to Jason.

Response H. A member of the Beef Industry Forum rings the website administrator to say that legal action might be taken if Jason's blogs continue to be published.

Responses A to D are open and fair. They engage in dialogue. They may be distressing to Jason, especially if the language is strong. But they are fair because they are either directly to Jason or in the same forum (blogs) that Jason used.

Responses E to H are not open and not fair. They are attempts to attack Jason or to prevent his views being heard, even though Helen and the Beef Industry Forum may feel personally under attack and feel that Jason has made incorrect claims. False claims, though — which might be felt to be "unfair" — are not the same as unfair methods of carrying out the dispute.

One of the most useful ways to decide whether one side in a dispute is attempting to suppress the other side is to see whether complaints have been made that affect the other side's ability to speak out. Complaints to superiors are a very common method of this sort.

Who is willing to discuss the issues? Another characteristic of suppression is avoidance of open discussion. Rather than welcoming an opportunity for dialogue and debate, the focus is put on the other person's behaviour or on official procedures. Alternatively, interaction is avoided altogether.

(Sometimes it is too dangerous to go straight to the person responsible for the problem — perhaps it is the boss! But this should not be a factor when the other person is a co-worker or a subordinate.)

***

These tests are helpful in determining what's going on, but are not foolproof. If you try applying the tests to cases you know a lot about, you'll learn to recognise the signals of fair play and the signals of suppression.

How the other side thinks

What about those who launch the attacks? They are the ones who harass their colleagues, make threats, issue disciplinary notices, dismiss employees and continue with damaging practices. It's easy to imagine that they are corrupt, scheming and just plain evil. Actually, this is not a useful way to think about it. How do they perceive the problem? How do they justify their behaviour?

From their point of view, the person who speaks out is at fault. The attackers usually think they have been remarkably restrained. They focus on the target's inadequacies (and who doesn't have some?) and on the real threat to the organisation caused by the person's unnecessary and destabilising claims.

In practice, what this means is that reprisals are never — absolutely never — called reprisals. Nearly always, these actions are justified in terms of the target's inadequacies and failures: their inability to do their job, their disloyalty, their violation of organisational norms, their paranoia.

Therefore, it is always best to assume that officials whom you think are corrupt and unscrupulous are actually, in their own minds, totally justified in everything they do. Perhaps there are a few people who say to themselves, "I'm dishonest and I'm going to victimise that honest person who's trying to expose me." But don't count on it!

Because each side believes it is correct, the struggle is one over credibility. Who will be believed?

Few books about bureaucracies provide much insight into these issues. One that does is Robert Jackall's *Moral Mazes: The World of Corporate Managers*. Jackall obtained access to a couple of big US corporations as well as a public relations firm. He spent many months interviewing managers and watching them in action, as well as reading many documents.

Jackall treated the world of corporate managers as a culture. He was like an anthropologist studying an alien tribe. His aim was to understand the social dynamics of corporate culture. He gives many case studies of activities and crises to illustrate his analysis.

Moral Mazes can be heavy-going at times, as some of the quotes below indicate. But it is worth persisting with the book because of the insights it offers. Here are some of Jackall's observations.

- Corporations are in a constant state of upheaval. When a new executive takes over a post, he (or occasionally she) brings in a whole new crew of cronies. Bureaucracy is a set of patronage networks.
- Corporations often respond to the whims and inclinations of the chief executive. Even an off-hand comment by the chief executive can trigger subordinates into frenzied activity to do what they think is being suggested. In many cases the result is ill-advised or disastrous.
- Conformity is enforced to amazingly fine details.
- Managers, to be successful, must continually adapt their personalities to fit the current situation. This is not just acting. They must become so natural at what they do that they "are" their act. Much of this adaptation is fitting in. Clothes must conform to expectations, but so must speech, attitudes and personal style. Those who don't adapt don't get ahead.
- Managers don't want to act until the decision is generally accepted. They experience a pervasive indecisiveness. Each one looks for signals on what decision will be favoured. Signals from the chief executive officer — the top boss — are especially important.
- Responsibility is diffused and hard to pin down. Managers avoid taking responsibility. The key thing is to avoid being blamed for a failure.
- Morality is doing what seems appropriate in the situation to get things done. Morality is doing what the boss wants. Having independent principles is a prescription for career stagnation or disaster.

- The symbolic manipulation of reality is pervasive. For any decision, managers discuss various reasons in order to settle on a way to give legitimacy for what the corporation does.
- Public relations is simply a tool. Truth is irrelevant.

The successful manager is one who can adapt to the prevailing ideas, who can please the boss, who can avoid being blamed for failure, and who can build alliances with supporters above and below.

Jackall devotes a chapter, "Drawing lines," to the corporation's response to whistleblowers. White was a health professional who tried to raise concern about hearing loss among many workers at a corporation's textile mills. He collected data and wrote a report. Due to his professional training and religious background, he felt this was a clear moral issue. But his attempts failed. He did not have supporters higher up. As well, his recommendations for change threatened powerful interests. Other managers felt uncomfortable with White's moral stance.

> Without clear authoritative sanctions, moral viewpoints threaten others within an organization by making claims on them that might impede their ability to read the drift of social situations. As a result, independent morally evaluative judgments get subordinated to the social intricacies of the bureaucratic workplace … Managers know that in the organization right and wrong get decided by those with enough clout to make their views stick. (p. 105).

White ended up leaving the company.

Brady was an accountant who found various discrepancies in a company's financial operations. At one stage,

Brady discussed the matter with a close friend, a man who had no defined position but considerable influence in the company and access to the highest circles in the organization. He was Mr. Fixit — a lobbyist, a front man, an all-around factotum, a man who knew how to get things done.

This friend took Brady's anonymous memorandum to a meeting of top figures in the corporation. "Immediately after the meeting, Brady's friend was fired and escorted from the building by armed guards." (p. 108). Brady now realised it was the chief executive himself who was fiddling the books. Brady was under suspicion of having written the memo. He eventually presented all his evidence to the company's chief lawyer, who wouldn't touch it. "Right after Brady's boss returned from Europe, Brady was summarily fired and he and his belongings were literally thrown out of the company building." (p. 109).

Nothing new here. Another whistleblower is dismissed. What is most interesting in Jackall's account is his description of how other managers saw the situation. They saw

> Brady's dilemma as devoid of moral or ethical content. In their view, the issues that Brady raises are, first of all, simply practical matters. His basic failing was, first, that he violated the fundamental rules of bureaucratic life. These are usually stated as a series of admonitions. (1) You never go around your boss. (2) You tell your boss what he wants to hear, even when your boss claims that he wants dissenting views. (3) If your boss wants something dropped, you drop it. (4) You are sensitive to your boss's wishes so that you anticipate what he wants; you don't force him, in other words, to act as boss. (5) Your job is not to report something that your boss does not want reported, but

rather to cover it up. You do what your job requires, and you keep your mouth shut. (pp. 109–110).

The second response of managers to Brady's case was that he had plenty of ways to justify not acting. Others obviously knew about the fiddling of the books but did nothing. They were all playing the game. Why should Brady worry about it? He would only make himself vulnerable.

The third response of managers was to say that those things that Brady got upset about — "irregular payments, doctored invoices, shuffling numbers in accounts" — were ordinary things in a corporation.

Moreover, as managers see it, playing sleight of hand with the monetary value of inventories, post- or pre-dating memoranda or invoices, tucking or squirreling large sums of money away to pull them out of one's hat at an opportune moment are all part and parcel of managing a large corporation where interpretations of performance, not necessarily performance itself, decide one's fate. (p. 110).

The fourth and final response of managers to Brady's case was to say that he shouldn't have acted on a moral code that had no relevance to the organisation.

Brady refused to recognize, in the view of the managers that I interviewed, that "truth" is socially defined, not absolute, and that therefore compromise, about anything and everything, is not moral defeat, as Brady seems to feel, but simply an inevitable fact of organizational life. They see this as the key reason why Brady's bosses did him in. And they too would do him in without any qualms. Managers, they say, do not want evangelists working for them. (p. 111).

After all these events, the chief executive — the one who fiddled the books — retired, elevated his loyal lieutenant to his former position and took an honorary position in the firm, as head of internal audit!

Concerning this case, Jackall concludes:

Bureaucracy transforms all moral issues into immediately practical concerns. A moral judgment based on a professional ethic makes little sense in a world where the etiquette of authority relationships and the necessity of protecting and covering for one's boss, one's network, and oneself supersede all other considerations and where nonaccountability for action is the norm. (p. 111).

Jackall's analysis is based on just a few US corporations. He had to approach dozens of corporations — and adapt his pitch — before he found a couple that granted access. There is no easy way of knowing which of his insights apply to other corporations, other types of bureaucracies, and in other countries. But in as much as the same sorts of dynamics occur, Jackall's examination shows that whistleblowers are up against something much bigger than a few corrupt individuals, or even a system of corruption.

The problem is the very structure of the organisation, in which managers who adapt to the ethos of pragmatism and who please their bosses are the ones who get ahead. To eliminate wrongdoing in corporations requires not just replacing or penalising a few individuals, but changing the entire organisational structure. It is the structure, within the wider corporate culture, that shapes the psychology of managers and creates the context for problems to occur.

Appendix: The language of exposing problems

The words we use have a great effect on the way we perceive the world. When people use the same words, often the meanings or associations are different. This applies to speaking out about problems.

The following table lists some words commonly used to refer to exposing a problem. The words depend partly on who reports the alleged problem to whom, and whether the exposure is done openly or covertly.

	open	*covert*
exposing equals or subordinates to those more powerful	reporting, dobbing, informing, snitching, whistleblowing	reporting, dobbing, informing, snitching, anonymous whistleblowing
exposing superiors to higher officials or outside authorities	whistleblowing	anonymous whistleblowing
exposing superiors or officials to the public	exposés, investigative journalism, social action, whistleblowing	leaking, anonymous whistleblowing

Reporting a classmate to a teacher is often called "dobbing" or "informing." Is the act of reporting bad just because people frown on "dobbing"? What if the classmate was raping a young child? Should reporting a burglar to police be called "informing"?

Judgements are often implied in our use of words. It's important to consider the actual act being referred to and not just the label.

4   Personal assessment: what should I do?

> Before acting, pause and reflect.
>
> - Check your assessment: hear the other side, get advice, examine your motives.
> - Clarify your personal goals.
> - Develop a strategy.

So there's a problem that needs attention. There are risks in speaking out, but the problem is urgent and it's worth taking the risks. So ... action! Right? Well, maybe not.

After finding out about a problem, it can be very tempting to act immediately. But unless you're very experienced and know exactly what's involved, it's wise to pause and reflect — indeed, pause and reflect several times.

Check your assessment of the problem

Some problems seem obvious enough: embezzlement, assault, hazardous practices. But it's best to be absolutely sure before launching into the issue. There are several ways to check.

Ask to hear the other side. This means talking to people who seem to be responsible for the problem. For example, if there seems to be a bias in appointments, ask to see the selection criteria and, if available, job applications. Talk to someone on the selection panel. There might actually be good reasons for the appointments.

Sometimes there are other explanations even for apparent cases of embezzlement, assault and hazardous practices. It may be, for example, that someone else wants to makes a person look bad.

It's remarkable how often people are willing to believe the worst about someone or something without talking to the people concerned. Some very nasty conflicts could be avoided by this simple precaution.

You notice that a company is selling outdated stock as if it were new. This could be a corrupt practice. It might also be because no one noticed.

When in doubt, it is better to assume incompetence or bad procedures rather than corruption and bad intentions. Very few organisations are perfectly efficient. Likewise, very few individuals are able to do everything they are supposed to.

… except in some cases. In a few cases, it can be risky to ask to hear the other side. It might show that you suspect something, and lead to an attack. It might also alert people so that they can cover up by hiding or destroying records, establishing cover stories and the like.

Robina Cosser comments

Don't alert the "other side," or they will launch a pre-emptive strike against you. Gather your evidence very, very quietly.

Sometimes your questions are quite innocent. You don't suspect anything. But just because you've asked about certain statements, accounts or events, perpetrators may think you know much more than you do. As a result, you may come under attack for no apparent reason.

If you do come under attack in such cases, that's a good indication that the problem is a serious one. But it's not a guarantee. It could be an attack for some other irrelevant reason.

Anyway, if it's risky to ask to hear the other side, you have to decide the best way to proceed. It might be safer to appear to be on a person's side. You might use an approach like this: "Someone was asking about the events last Thursday. I'm sure there's not *really* any problem. Can you suggest the best way to explain the situation to them?" If you suspect the worst, this is a bit devious. A more direct approach is, "I'm concerned about what happened on Thursday. I'd like to hear your explanation." If you are known for being straightforward — in other words, blunt — this may be okay.

In some cases, though, it is not effective to ask to hear the other side. If you have solid evidence of major fraud by top management, raising your concerns is a mistake. You could be dismissed on the spot and a cover-up initiated immediately.

Get independent advice. To determine whether your assessment is sensible, it can be very helpful to talk to someone who's not involved. Describe the case to them and present the evidence you have. Ask whether there could be an innocent explanation. Also ask whether they think the issue is as serious as you think it is.

For example, there have been several incidents that you think reveal pervasive racist attitudes, though the employer officially opposes racism. Is your interpretation reasonable, or are you exaggerating the significance of the incidents? Even if there is a serious problem, is there enough evidence from these incidents to really show it?

The sort of person who can give the most helpful independent advice should be balanced, concerned, sympathetic, honest and totally trustworthy. They should be able to give a *balanced* assessment, not being too biased for or against anyone involved, and not being distorted due to passionate views on certain issues. They should be *concerned* about problems such as corruption or racism or whatever. If they don't care about the problem, they are hardly in a position to tell whether it's really serious. They should be reasonably *sympathetic* to you personally, enough to be willing to help you be as effective as possible. They should be *honest*, which means willing to tell you what they really think even if they think you're wrong. Finally, they should be totally *trustworthy*. You don't want anyone repeating your private concerns to all and sundry, including those you suspect of causing the problem.

There are few people who are ideal in all these respects. Finding someone who is both sympathetic and honest is difficult enough. But you don't have to find a perfect person. Just find someone who is reasonably good and who has time to help.

How to find someone? The best way is by asking around and going by a person's reputation. If others say someone is honest and discreet, that's a good recommendation.

If the independent person supports your view, well and good. If not, then you need to reconsider. Are you still convinced there's a serious problem? If so, then you might contact another independent person. The first person might have a bias you don't know about.

If you've been to several independent people and none of them thinks your concerns are warranted, it's time for a rethink. Perhaps you are imagining a problem where none exists. Perhaps it's better to wait a while. Even if there's a serious problem, you have little chance of doing anything about it if you can't convince independent people. Maybe you need more evidence.

Robina Cosser comments

Sometimes it is better not to discuss it with anybody, especially if you live in a small town, where everyone has worked with, wants to work with, is a member of a club with or is a relative of everybody else.

Harold used to work in banks and, since leaving, began investigating corruption in the banking industry. However, his investigations were hampered in various ways. Some of his documents disappeared, people refused to talk to him and he suspected that there was constant surveillance of his movements. He then approached several independent people for their assessment. While sympathetic, they said more evidence was needed, both of corruption and of surveillance. Harold remains convinced that both are occurring.

Examine your motives When you call attention to a problem, in principle it shouldn't matter what your motives are. After all, if there's a danger to public health, the key thing is to address it. So what if there's a promotion involved for the person who exposes it?

In practice, motives are important. If your reason for acting is personal advancement or status, that may distort your view of what the most serious problems are.

You discover that the boss has been tolerating minor pilfering from the storehouse. If the boss goes, you are next in line for her position. How does that affect your perception of the seriousness of the issue?

More importantly, if your motives are suspect, you may not be as effective in acting against the problem. The reason is that people will attribute your actions to your self-interest.

> ### Cynthia Kardell comments
>
> If your primary concern is the motivation of the wrongdoer and your aim is to have them punished, you are likely to be seen as malicious and your complaint seen as vexatious and brushed aside. Instead, focus on what was actually done and allow others to come to the same conclusions as you.

However, if no one ever acted except with the purest of motives, then not much would ever be accomplished. Some situations are so corrupt that everyone is tainted. In a corrupt police force, sometimes the best people to expose the problems are police who have been involved themselves. Even if your motive is to escape corruption charges, your willingness to speak out can be a valuable social service.

A warning

If you are compromised by your participation in unsavoury practices, you may be in special danger of being victimised. Some compromised whistleblowers are attacked out of all proportion to what they've done, while the most corrupt individuals escape unscathed. On the other hand, being spotless is no guarantee of safety. Some whistleblowers who are totally innocent of any wrongdoing have been framed for major crimes.

Clarify your personal goals

After checking that your assessment of the problem is correct, it's time to decide your goals. That may seem obvious enough. Fix the problem. Justice. Get everything working the way it ought to.

Clarifying personal goals has to be more precise than this. It needs to include what you'd like to achieve for yourself and towards fixing the problem, and what costs you're willing to bear.

Start by being as precise as possible about your goals.

- Is it to ensure that key decision makers know about a problem?
- Is it to publicise the situation so lots of people know about it?
- Is it to rectify a particular situation?
- Is it to transform an entire organisation?
- Is it to expose wrongdoers?
- Is it to subject wrongdoers to appropriate penalties?
- Is it to obtain or regain an appropriate position for yourself?
- Is it to obtain compensation for the injustices you've suffered?
- Is it to obtain personal satisfaction that you've done what you can?

In many cases your goals are mixtures of things, for example fixing the problem, penalising the wrongdoers and obtaining compensation. Try to separate out the different components. Which ones are most important to you? Is it more important to prevent future problems or to bring wrongdoers to justice?

Try to be even more specific. If you want to publicise the situation, would a notice to all employees be sufficient? What about an article in the local newspaper? If you want something personally, what exactly would suffice? A formal apology? A payment? How much?

It can be difficult to clarify goals, but it's important. In many cases individuals spend months or years pursuing a case only to find that they are dissatisfied with the outcome. That's often because their underlying goals were different from what they thought — or because they never thought carefully about their goals and so didn't have a hope of achieving them.

Being specific about goals is a crucial first step. Another vital step is to try to be realistic. If your goal is to transform the organisation, that's possibly a lifetime task. Even to expose wrongdoing can be a major operation.

The costs of seeking change are often much greater and longer lasting than imagined. What seems like it should take six months can take six years. There can be vast financial costs. But even more serious are the health and emotional costs. Your health may suffer from the stress of the process, and your closest relationships may be strained or broken. More details are given in chapter 11, including advice on reducing these consequences.

To work out the likely impacts, think of the worst scenario that seems possible. Then multiply the costs — time, money, health, emotions — by ten. Yes, things could be mighty tough!

By adopting wise strategies and precautions, you can reduce the harmful consequences. Who knows, you might be one of the exceedingly lucky ones who comes out of the process better off than before.

Lots of people think their case is so good that they can't lose. That's an illusion. It's far better to be prepared for the worst. That way you will be ready when things get really difficult.

Cynthia Kardell comments

You need to be able to recognise success when it happens, because you rarely get everything you want, and it never comes in the form that you wanted or first anticipated.

Build a strategy

A strategy is essentially a plan for getting something done — a plan that takes into account where you are to start with, what resources you have and what obstacles you face, and where you're trying to go. If you're going to be successful, developing a strategy can make a big difference. A fire brigade or a sporting team without a plan can only succeed by being lucky, and the same applies to others.

Let's look at things in terms of a movement from the present to the future. We are in a certain situation now; we take various actions and use various methods; we end up in some other situation down the track.

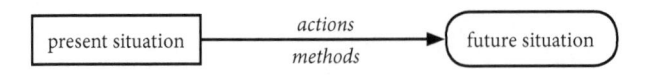

| present situation | —— *actions* / *methods* ——▶ | future situation |

We don't control everything about this process, of course. Other people get in the way with their own actions, and there are all sorts of other factors, including opportunities, constraints (time, money, resources), interactions between people and pure chance. In order to do the best we can, we need to understand and plan. This can be thought of this way:

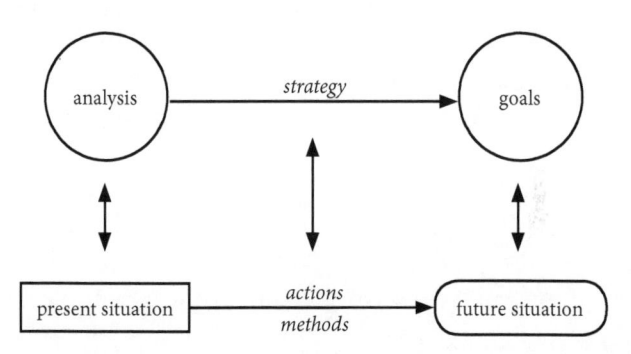

```
    ( analysis ) ──strategy──▶ ( goals )
        ↕              ↕           ↕
  [present situation] ──actions──▶ [future situation]
                        methods
```

In this diagram, the bottom level — from present to future situation — involves what actually happens. The top level — analysis, strategy, goals — involves thinking about what happens.

Analysis is what we do to understand the present situation. It's valuable to know, for example, how an organisation operates, what your own skills and resources are, and who your likely supporters and opponents are. To carry out an analysis, you can study books on organisational theory, ask knowledgeable people and build a mental model of your own about how society operates.

Analysis, if taken seriously, is an enormous task. Many scholars spend their whole careers undertaking an analysis of some small facet of social life. What you need is an analysis oriented to practical action. You don't need to know things for their intellectual value, but rather so you can figure out what's likely to happen when you do something.

Goals are what you want to achieve. If you're going to get there, you need to know what they are. As discussed earlier, clarifying your goals is vital. There's a danger in spending too much time on analysis and not enough on clarifying goals.

Strategy is your plan for going from present to future. It can be considered to be an analysis of actions and methods. It builds on your analysis of the present situation and takes into account your goals for the future. It includes planning for contingencies. Developing an effective strategy is vital.

Elaine, a doctor at a hospital, is concerned that there are far too many referrals for a procedure using an expensive scanner, when actually a simple visual examination would do in most cases. She thinks this is because of pressures to justify the expense of the scanner. As part of her analysis of the situation, she finds that some medical researchers at the hospital hold a patent on the scanner and are pushing strongly for its use. Also, many other doctors are generally in favour of high-technology medicine. Her specific goal is to have a formal reassessment of the value of the scanner. A more general goal is to reduce the bias in favour of highly expensive medical equipment. She decides to circulate a memo asking for a comparison of the scanner versus visual examination.

To her surprise, she is personally attacked at the next staff meeting for questioning the scanner. She also starts receiving excessive scrutiny from one particular senior doctor, and is assigned to less pleasant and less stimulating rounds. After talking to a few others — only some of whom are sympathetic — she decides to lie low for a while, collect more information about the scanner and its effectiveness, and to contact a local medical consumers group. (And so on.)

Elaine's initial strategy was circulating a memo, which seemed reasonable in the situation. When that didn't work, she reassessed the situation — more analysis. In fact, the response to her memo revealed a lot about the dynamics of the hospital. Sometimes action is the best way to find out how things really operate. Elaine is now trying a new strategy. She may also reassess her goals in the light of her further experiences.

This example illustrates an important point: analyses, strategies and goals need to be regularly examined and updated. You might decide to continue as before, but you need to be open to change.

Cynthia Kardell comments

Get to know your enemy. Learn from what they've done. Learn about how they usually respond and take it into account before you take a step. It's a bit like a chess game, in which you plan ahead and make moves that counter likely moves by your opponent. Find a buddy to strategise with.

One of the hardest things is to know when to stop. After spending two years in a court battle, should you agree to a settlement? After battling the organisation for five years, should you resign and leave? These are difficult sorts of decisions. They need to be made.

One way to think about this is to look at the "opportunity cost" of your activities. If you weren't battling the organisation, you might instead be spending your time working somewhere else, and perhaps helping to achieve the same or different goals. There is a "cost" in

ONE OF LIFE'S DEFINING MOMENTS....

Australian whistleblower Kevin Lindeberg drew this cartoon to illustrate that "social justice agencies" do not welcome whistleblowers.

your present activities, namely not taking up other opportunities, or in other words doing different things.

To get an insight into this, think of the most general formulation of your goals. Are they to achieve personal satisfaction, or help promote accountability? Then think of other strategies — other jobs, other campaigns, other places — to achieve these goals. Your task is the same: to work out the best strategy for your own life.

5 Preparation

> Before taking action, prepare.
>
> - Document the problem: letters, photos, recordings, statements ...
> - Know the context (consult well-informed people, consult research findings).
> - Propose solutions.
> - Get advice and support: family, friends, co-workers, others.

Document the problem

Documenting the problem is the foundation of success. Without documentation, you have to depend on other people backing you — and all too often they won't. With documentation, you at least have a chance.

Theresa, an experienced worker, was a bit disturbed to hear from her boss at a staff meeting that a contract had been given to the Smith Consultancy without an open bidding process, but she set aside her doubts when the urgency and special requirements were explained.

The next week it was reported in the press that the Smith Consultancy had been charged with various crimes including bribery. She confronted her boss about it, only to be told that she must have misheard him — they had only been considering giving the contract to Smith's. Her co-workers either refused to talk about it or said the boss must be right.

For evidence to have credibility, usually it must be in permanent form.

Letters, memos, reports. These are the core of most documentation. Ensure that you have copies of anything that might be useful. Sometimes written records are self-explanatory, but often it is helpful to keep notes of any necessary information. For example, if a document doesn't have a date, add a note saying when you received it.

You can create your own records too. If you've just been to an important meeting, it can be useful to write a letter to the convenor summarising what happened. "Helen — Just to confirm, at today's meeting it was agreed that I would head a task force …"

Cynthia Kardell comments

Don't send documents from work to your home address, as your messages can be traced. In fact, when collecting documents, don't use your employer's email or other communication systems from the time you find evidence of wrongdoing, because they could find out what you're up to before you want them to know. Even worse, they could reprimand or dismiss you for using work resources for an improper (non-work) purpose.

Photos. Sometimes a picture is worth a thousand words, for example in cases of environmental damage or physical assault. But pictures don't usually explain their context. It's vital to record the date, time, location, photographer, and any other relevant information. If possible, have another person verify the information.

Recordings. A recording is a powerful challenge to people who claim they didn't say something. As in the case of photos, record the time, location and other details.

Diaries. If you are caught up in a difficult situation, keeping a diary is an excellent idea. You should record any events of significance, giving time, place, situation, people present and your interpretation of what happened. A diary is far more accurate than memories if you ever need to check the sequence of events or determine who told you something first. You can write as much as you like, but a brief summary is quite sufficient: "Friday 19 October 2012: Just after arriving at work at 8.30, Fred told me that three of us — him, Cath and me — would be carpeted because of the leak about the budget blowout." A diary is also an excellent way to get some of the worry out of your system.

Statements by witnesses. Since witnesses can leave or change their minds about what they saw or heard, getting a statement can be a good idea. If you have just attended a crucial meeting where a shady practice was discussed or where an unscrupulous attack was made on you or someone else, write your own statement and try to get others to sign it, for example saying "This is an accurate account of what occurred." (Note that if you ever need to use a witness statement, this potentially makes the witness vulnerable to reprisals.)

Sunil had been calling for an open and accountable process for granting building licences, as there had long been suspicions about bias in the process. As a result, his work had come under intense scrutiny by the department head. He was prepared when he was called to a meeting with the head to talk about his performance. In a previous job, he had been caught unawares in a gruelling dressing down by three managers. This time he took along a co-worker as a witness — someone known to be honest and no one's pawn. He also took along a tape recorder and asked to record the meeting. The head said he hoped it wouldn't be necessary. The meeting was a low-key affair. Afterwards, Sunil wrote a letter to the head summarising what had been said, and had his witness sign a copy.

***

How much documentation is enough? Probably more than what you have! Often it's better to lie low and collect more evidence rather than risk a premature disclosure. The bigger and more serious the problem, the more evidence you need. In the case of deep-rooted corruption, for example, you need enough material to counter highly determined efforts to deny the problem, including:

- destruction of documents
- systematic lying
- manufacture of false documents
- elaborate frame-ups.

Documents are the foundation of your case, but no one likes ploughing through a giant pile of paper. You also need to write a concise summary to put everything into context. There's more on this in chapter 9.

It is wise to keep copies of crucial documents in a secure place. If your only copies are all in a file in your office, you might find them missing one morning — or even find that you've been fired and locked out of your office. If you're a community activist, your documents could be taken in a burglary. So keep copies in a location besides your usual one, plus perhaps with a trusted friend or legal adviser.

Jean Lennane

advises having at least four copies in different locations, in case of a raid. She says the key thing to protect is evidence. If in doubt about the relevance of a document, keep it plus copies.

What risks should you take to obtain documents? This is a difficult question. It raises legal and ethical issues. In many situations it is a violation of the law or formal policy to make copies of documents, take them off the premises or show them to outsiders. If you are caught violating procedures, you could be sued or dismissed. This could happen even if lots of people violate the same procedures. Selective attack is the essence of victimisation.

If the documents reveal a multimillion dollar scam or a serious hazard to health, then you may consider that you are justified in violating the law. This is especially the case if the main effect of the regulations is to prevent public scrutiny and cover up corruption. On the other hand, there might be other ethical factors involved. For example, the documents might include personal details about clients or patients. There are, after all, some good reasons for confidentiality of documents. To choose the most appropriate course of action, you need to use your judgement and to obtain advice from people you can trust.

What about making recordings surreptitiously? You can buy tiny recorders that enable you to audio-record conversations and meetings unobtrusively. In some jurisdictions, secret recordings are illegal, such as some recordings of telephone conversations. But more important than this is the effect on the way people will react to you if they find out you have recorded conversations without telling them. Basically, they will trust you less, perhaps not at all. That's a serious consequence.

For ordinary purposes, secret recording is not a good idea, especially if you hope to continue interacting with the same people. It may be warranted in the case of serious corruption, such as undercover operations against corrupt police or in the case of serious harassment. If you don't intend remaining at a job, the impact on your relations with co-workers may not be so important.

Know the context

It is extremely valuable to be able to put your own situation in context. That means comparing it to similar situations and comparing the nature of the problems and the types of solutions proposed.

Maria was new to the job. She was disturbed when Jonah, a senior co-worker, made sexual jokes, stood close to her and touched her on the arm and shoulder and asked her out for dinner. She wasn't sure whether to avoid him or file a complaint. She talked to other women who worked with Jonah and also read some books on sexual harassment. She decided that she'd have to be firm with Jonah — she told him to cut the jokes and give her some more space and that she wanted to keep their relationship professional. They got on fine after that. Maria also warned other new workers what to expect.

In other cases, the problem turns out to be more serious. Then it's time to start documenting everything.

In the case of large-scale problems, you need to find out how pervasive they are, whether others are aware of them and whether

Jean Lennane (in white) and other members of Whistleblowers Australia on the steps of the New South Wales parliament in 1997, after the parliamentary review of the Independent Commission Against Corruption.

anyone is trying to do anything about them. It is sensible to join others, or to get their support if you decide to take action.

Alexi worked in the subsidiary of a multinational corporation. He noticed that the subsidiary was buying inputs from the parent at inflated prices and selling back output at unrealistic discounts. The result was the subsidiary made no money, thereby reducing its taxes. This benefited the corporation overall but starved the government where the subsidiary was based. Alexi was concerned about the manipulation even if it was technically legal. He started investigating and found that this system of transfer payments to avoid tax was commonplace among multinationals and that some governments and consumer groups were trying to do something about it.

There are several good ways to learn about the context.

Talk to experienced and knowledgeable people — old-timers with long memories. Often they can provide insights unavailable any other way. As well, they may be able to tell you about other attempts to change things — and what happened to the would-be reformers. Did they suffer reprisals, quit trying, or end up being rewarded?

Talk to campaigners — people who are taking action about social problems. They often have a really good grasp of why things happen the way they do. If you are concerned that unemployment figures are being fiddled to make politicians look good, talk to activists who deal with jobs, poverty or social justice.

Find out if anyone has done research into the area. This could be academics, investigative journalists or independent investigators. If you're concerned about the oil industry, ask at the local university or media outlet for the person who knows the most about it. When you find someone who knows something about the topic, ask them to recommend the most knowledgeable people in the region or country. People researching a topic usually know who are the top people in the field. This is the quickest way to tap into relevant expertise — or to find out that there isn't any.

Undertake your own investigation. You can find out what has been written already by going through library catalogues and indexes and the Internet. Librarians can help you get started. If you don't know much about doing investigations, you may be able to find an academic, a good student or an independent researcher who is willing to help you.

If your goal is doing something about the problem, then learning about the context is not a goal in itself, but just a way to improve your chance of success. You are looking for insights that are practical: they should give you a better idea of what to do and what not to do. Be wary of academics who only provide intellectual insights, which are all very well for scholarly journals and conferences but not much use otherwise. Be wary of journalists or activists who want to use you for their own purposes — a story or a campaign — without concern about your own goals.

Lesley Pinson comments

It is extremely important that a person who has blown the whistle — or who is contemplating blowing it — learns as much as they can. Understanding as much as possible helps to minimise the confusion whistleblowers feel and maximises the individual's ability to make the best decision about tactics. "Information is power."

Propose solutions

Documenting and exposing the problem is vital, but what then? If the problem is revealed, does that mean that powerholders will "do the right thing" and fix it? Hardly. There are several standard responses.

1. Complaints and complainants are ignored. A powerful establishment can tolerate a bit of dissent, as long as no one takes much notice.
2. Complainants are attacked. If the complaints become too loud or are taken seriously by too many people, an attack on the complainants is mounted.
3. Reassuring statements are made. If the pressure is too great to ignore or suppress, then the problem may be acknowledged and said to be being dealt with. Often this is just public relations.
4. Procedures are changed so it is harder to detect and document the problem.
5. A few superficial improvements are made. To ease the pressure, some new policies might be announced or a few individuals sacrificed — but the situation is really unchanged.
6. Steps are taken that genuinely reduce the problem.

Most challengers never get past responses 1 and 2. But if enough pressure can be mounted, there is a chance of real change. The biggest risk is getting stuck with responses 3, 4 or 5. Your aim is to push past these to response 6.

One way to help achieve response 6 is to propose solutions as well as highlight problems. The solution needs to be challenging yet achievable. It should be realistic and sound sensible. It should be difficult to fake.

As an experienced accountant with a successful career in several industries, Enrico discovered a massive insurance fraud. He fed information to a small but effective consumer group with links to a few trusted politicians. As a result of publicity, the government set up a commission of inquiry into the industry. The commission was better than most. Several top corporate figures lost their jobs (and later were quietly employed elsewhere). The commission made some bland recommendations, but no laws were passed — the industry had some powerful political friends.

Enrico was far more effective than others before him, half a dozen of whom had given up or lost their jobs after speaking out. But Enrico and his allies needed to tie their exposure of the fraud with specific suggestions for how to fix it — such as legal provision for oversight with consumer-group input and public interest disclosure clauses in employment contracts.

It seems to be asking a lot of someone to not only expose a problem but also come up with a solution. Surely it's enough just to reveal the problem! Although it is extremely challenging to come up with an appropriate solution, this is a good discipline. Thinking through the sorts of solutions that would be satisfactory and saleable can be helpful in deciding the best way to document and expose the problem. Best of all, there may be a way to package together a problem and a solution.

Obtain advice and support

Before embarking, it is absolutely vital to obtain advice and support. This applies whether you are approaching someone you think copied your work inappropriately or whether you are tackling organised crime.

Family. Talk to everyone you live with or are close to, including partner, parents, children and siblings. Explain what you know and what you're planning to do — and what might happen. If they are willing to back you, then you are in a *much* stronger position. If they are strongly opposed to your plans, you need to think again. In this situation, there is no right or wrong decision. You need to weigh up the likely consequences in light of your own values.

Remember also that in some cases family members may come under attack because of your stand. If you are publicly attacked, perhaps even framed, then your children might be scorned at school or your sister could be threatened with losing her job. Even short of these consequences, your family will be greatly affected by what happens to you: enormous stress, loss of career opportunities, perhaps unemployment.

On the other hand, standing up for what you believe can be enormously empowering. Self-respect and mutual respect can make up for a lot of other losses.

Friends. Talk to those you trust the most. But be aware that many "friends" may turn away if you change. They wish you wouldn't talk so much about the problems of embezzlement, drug cover-ups or paedophilia. They'd prefer watching sport or talking about the kids — "lighten up," they might say. If you take a strong stand on an issue, you may lose some friends but gain others.

When you become really involved in the issues, friends and family can be helpful in giving an outsider's viewpoint. It's easy to become obsessed with details and lose sight of the overall picture. Ask for advice on how to present your ideas. But don't overstep the mark by letting your concerns dominate the relationship.

Friends who are sympathetic can be very helpful. They may have contacts, skills and sage advice.

Try to sense when you are straining the relationship. If your best friend asks for more details, proceed. If she repeatedly tries to change the subject, that's a different signal.

Co-workers. Co-workers may be your friends too, but their commitment is not likely to be as high. Don't be surprised if many of them turn away when the heat is on.

Nevertheless, maintaining good relationships with at least some co-workers is extremely valuable. They can give you feedback about how others see your actions, and what impact your initiatives are having. You don't need to ask them to support you. Some may volunteer to do that. But just maintaining open channels of communication is important.

The more sensitive the issue, and the less public your role, the more caution is needed in confiding with co-workers. Some of them may go straight to the boss with everything you say — not to mention a few exaggerations for good measure!

Trade unions and professional associations. If your union or association is behind you, you have a powerful ally indeed. But don't count on support. Many union officials are unwilling to tackle management on anything except narrow industrial issues. They may not act unless there is overwhelming support from the membership — and sometimes not even then! Some union officials are tools of management, or just hope to obtain a promotion by not rocking the boat.

Get to know your union officials and study their track records. If it's a principled union or you know the right people, you may be able to get support — and that is a tremendous advantage. But be prepared for little or no support. Even worse, the union may actively oppose you.

Isla MacGregor

Isla MacGregor comments

Some union officials don't want to support whistleblowers because in doing so they might attract attention to their own organisation's lack of accountability or democratic process. Some senior management people, particularly in the public sector, deliberately join unions to frustrate attempts by co-workers to enlist support of unions in discrimination and victimisation disputes or public interest disclosures.

Lesley Pinson comments

Remember that if you are complaining about the activities of co-workers, they may also be union members, so your union may have a conflict in providing support.

Cynthia Kardell comments

If union officials are less than supportive, keep your complaints about the union to yourself and learn to use them, as and when you need to — just don't rely on them. When it is all over, then consider raising your complaints.

Others. There are lots of others you can contact to obtain advice and support. This includes social activists, journalists, politicians, lawyers and many others. This is discussed further in chapter 9.

Lesley Pinson comments

It is useful to seek legal advice as early as possible. Although this might involve a financial outlay, it could save greater costs if you later end up with legal problems that could have been avoided.

You are also well advised to keep your doctor informed about what you are proposing to do. S/he might be able to advise useful stress management techniques and will be better able to attest to your sanity and stress-related symptoms, should this ever be necessary.

Many whistleblowers have postponed seeking legal or medical advice until far too late, typically only when they have serious legal or medical problems. They then have unrealistic expectations that their lawyers and doctors will be able to fix their problems. It is also useful and empowering to know you have the support of a sympathetic lawyer and doctor, should you need it.

Cynthia Kardell comments

If what unions and lawyers are asking you to do leaves you feeling cornered and scared, with tightness in your chest, say no to whatever is being asked of you and say you will need some time to think it through. Then get advice from someone you can trust to think it through with you, make a choice and stick with it.

You've made a careful assessment of the problem and what you can do about it (chapters 2 to 4). You've collected more documents than you know what to do with, studied the situation at length, formulated a solution and obtained advice from various sources (this chapter). What next? There are four main approaches. You can use low-profile operations (chapter 6), proceed through official channels (chapter 7), make anonymous disclosures (chapter 8) or build support (chapter 9) — or some combination of these.

6 Low-profile operations

> You can seek to address a problem by talking to people, introducing ideas, encouraging discussion and fostering awareness — and doing it inconspicuously.

Is it possible to help get a problem fixed while keeping a low profile? Sometimes it is and, if so, it's definitely worth trying. Your task is to figure out how the system works and talk to people in ways that encourage them to do things differently. Most commonly this is inside an organisation.

The basic elements of this strategy are:

- understand the organisation, the people and the possibilities for change
- know your own situation and skills
- sow subtle seeds for change.

The following cases illustrate some of the ways to go about this.

Bob's boss was starting to set a bad example. The boss would boast about the success of the department while ignoring indications of impending disaster — in particular, service standards in some areas were falling, with serious impacts on a few clients. Bob wanted to change this trend but was wary about speaking out because the boss did not welcome bad news about performance. Bob needed to act without making himself a target.

So whenever someone fixed a problem in a weak area, Bob — when talking quietly with the boss, or in a casual group situation — said it was wonderful what his co-worker had done in preventing a bigger problem later on. Bob used the boss's rhetoric and style but with a slightly different orientation. Furthermore, Bob was able to get the boss to take credit for this new orientation. Bob's subtle interventions changed a trend that could have been disastrous, without anyone really noticing he had done anything.

Alan started working in a non-profit organisation where most of the other workers knew each other well. Alan quickly learned that appointments and promotions were based on who you knew, not how well you did your job, and this meant some workers were allowed to abuse their positions, for example running personal businesses during working hours. Alan sought out a senior, well-respected member of the organisation, Heloise, and talked to her about the issues, introducing some ideas about best-practice appointment procedures. Heloise started asking questions and mentioning some of these ideas, but in a way that didn't offend anyone: everyone knew Heloise had the best interests of the organisation at heart. As a result of Heloise's suggestions to experiment with different procedures, several new workers were appointed from outside the traditional narrow circle, and gradually the complacent culture began to change.

Ngu worked in a light manufacturing plant, and noticed lots of breaches of safety regulations. Having seen others lose their jobs for making formal complaints, Ngu started a rumour — based on truth — about a competing plant that had received a surprise safety inspection, passed with merit and subsequently been awarded lucrative contracts. The rumour spread to management and led to improvements. Ngu then started a rumour — also based on truth — that morale and productivity had improved due to pride over safety-consciousness. (Ngu knew that false rumours could end up making things worse.)

Sally was an active member of her church, and became concerned about a shift in emphasis from meekness and charity to snobbery and arrogance towards people of other nationalities and religions. Sally was already known for circulating "interesting reading" — articles she found on the Internet, with her own brief commentaries — to a church email list. She occasionally chose items highlighting issues of religion and intolerance and other problems she saw emerging in her church. Some of these stimulated discussion and led to an atmosphere of opinion in favour of the church's traditional orientation.

Tal worked in a unit whose top managers were giving themselves unwarranted privileges — extra-large offices, first-class air travel, generous expense accounts — despite declining performance. These displays of privilege undermined morale as well as costing the firm. Tal was in touch with a nearby university that regularly carried out studies in conjunction with the unit. Tal found a receptive academic and suggested a type of mild "action research" involving asking questions of all staff in the unit. The questions were ostensibly about surveying opinions but actually drew attention to the privileges of managers, contrasting them to the stated values of the firm. The research project stimulated awareness among several of the staff so that spending priorities were put on the planning agenda, leading to some restraint in the executive behaviour.

Heidi worked in a large law office. She discovered that two senior lawyers were taking credit for her work and billing clients multiple times for it. She considered making a complaint but realised she would probably be sidelined or lose her job as a result. Instead, she continued her careful work and began regularly giving updates and copies to her boss and several others so it would be harder for the two lawyers to misuse it. She quietly warned her boss about the risk to the firm if clients discovered any fraud. The two partners found they couldn't so easily use Heidi's work for their personal advantage. One of them retired and the other took a different job.

These are examples of how members of an organisation can try to bring about change in small, subtle ways. To do this effectively requires a good understanding of the organisation and the people in it, plus skills in intervening.

- Bob used his interpersonal skills to influence his boss.
- Alan chose to influence Heloise, an opinion leader.
- Ngu raised ideas via truth-based rumours.
- Sally introduced ideas via articles she circulated.
- Tal fostered awareness by involving outsiders in a questioning process.
- Heidi protected herself and gained support by providing information to others, especially her boss.

Advantages

Low-profile operations are relatively low risk, compared to complaining to the boss or an external agency. This means reprisals are far less likely. This is a major advantage.

Raising ideas in a low-key fashion sometimes can be more effective in bringing about change, because people are less resistant: they are not being personally challenged, but rather encouraged to see things in a different way. In contrast, a formal complaint often puts others into conflict mode, thinking in terms of defence, counter-attack or damage control rather than enabling change.

With low-profile operations, the focus is more on issues than the person raising them. There is less attention to the individual and more on what's happening. This is actually what whistleblowers want but seldom achieve.

Because these sorts of operations are low risk, it's usually possible to stay in the job and try again. Becoming successful at low-profile operations is an acquired skill: practice is vital. Some people have a head start, learning these sorts of skills in their family, school or prior workplaces. Even so, anyone can acquire greater skill in a relatively safe way.

Low-profile operations can provide a model for others. Some co-workers may understand exactly what is happening and, assuming they approve, assist the operations or undertake some of their own. Others may not realise that these sorts of operations are occurring, but nevertheless be influenced by the atmosphere in the workplace in which managers show some receptivity to change without major interventions. If a cultural shift can occur towards greater self-awareness about processes, standards and integrity, this is the most positive outcome.

With all these advantages, you might think the low-profile route is definitely the way to go. But there are shortcomings too.

Disadvantages

Sometimes problems are deeply entrenched. For example, corruption might be pervasive or bosses might be set in their ways. In many such circumstances, low-profile attempts at change simply won't work. They are too weak to make any difference. They might be worth trying just to be sure, but if it's apparent that problems are not going to be shifted this way, it's a waste of time and effort to persist with this approach.

Sometimes you are not the right person to achieve low-profile change. It might be the boss has singled you out for scrutiny, so anything you do is treated with suspicion. If the boss is threatened by your presence or contributions, then suggesting change might actually be counterproductive: the boss might be perverse and do the opposite. (However, this might open options for suggesting the opposite of what you want.) Perhaps you are so junior that your efforts are totally ignored. Perhaps the organisation has a sort of initiation, formal or informal, and until you have passed it, your efforts are in vain. Getting yourself into a position of some potential influence might be so difficult or compromising or slow that it's not worth the effort.

If you have already spoken out about problems, it may be too late for low-profile operations. If you're seen as a troublemaker, your interventions will be treated with suspicion. The best person to foster change within the system is someone who is a trusted member of the team, and if you've been outspoken this may not be you.

In some places, there are so many reorganisations and changes in personnel that it's not easy to exert any influence. All your careful work in building relationships and suggesting ideas is overturned in an instant when a new managerial team is installed and new procedures introduced. In a turbulent environment, it is still possible to have an influence, but different skills are required: the key is to intervene in the ongoing change process. However, if the change is driven by outside pressures, such as markets, intervention might be only a rear-guard effort.

Another constraint is shortage of time. You might have a challenging job and have little spare time to devote to fostering change.

You might be doing worthwhile things in your job. Diverting some of your energy to low-profile operations might not be the best use of your capabilities.

It might be that you have few skills and little interest in low-profile operations. Some workers are oriented to doing a technical job and may not be comfortable trying to change things via interpersonal interactions — it might feel manipulative. Furthermore, if you have no enthusiasm for this sort of approach, you may bungle it.

Imagine, on the other hand, that you are a sophisticated practitioner of the arts of fostering change through seeding ideas and building relationships. You might become frustrated because some of your co-workers are trying to achieve the same goals but making a mess of it by taking rash actions, antagonising the boss, telling everyone what you are trying to do, or in other ways spoiling the ground with premature, inept and counterproductive actions. To succeed in such a situation, you will need to be very skilled indeed!

Conclusion

It can be very worthwhile to address problems through low-profile operations. Anyone thinking of making a complaint, especially a formal complaint, should think first about how they might bring about change with much less visibility. As discussed in the next chapter, formal complaints are far less likely to be effective than most people imagine. Low-profile operations might seem too small and too slow — but they still might be better than the alternatives.

However, there are many circumstances in which this approach is not suitable. The problems might be too entrenched and you might not be in the right situation or have the time or skills to have an impact. Figuring out how you can be effective is vital.

The news is filled with stories about major problems in organisations, and occasionally there are stories about courageous whistleblowers. In contrast, low-profile operations are hardly ever reported. Some of the most skilled practitioners have a significant influence without others even being aware of what they have done. Their work is behind the scenes, and all the more effective by being invisible. So do not discount this option. The world is a better place because of the many people who bring about change in low-profile ways.

7 Official channels

- Whistleblowers seldom get much satisfaction from official channels such as internal grievance procedures, government agencies or the courts.
- Official channels seldom deliver justice because they narrow the issues and don't have enough resources or willpower to take on powerful offenders.
- To make a decision about which official channels to use, list possible options, investigate promising ones and weigh up their likely benefits and costs.
- Improve your chances of winning by learning about the process, polishing your submissions and choosing your advocates carefully.

There are all sorts of ways you can try to get a response, or obtain justice, through established procedures. Some possible channels are:

- Bosses, senior managers, chief executive officers
- Boards of management or trustees

- Internal grievance procedures
- Shareholders' meetings
- Professional association procedures
- Ombudsmen
- Regulatory agencies
- Antidiscrimination bodies
- Anticorruption bodies
- Auditors-general or inspectors general
- Government departments
- Politicians
- Parliamentary hearings
- Commissions of inquiry
- Courts

Within each of these categories, there may be many variations. When operating as an employee within an organisation, a typical first step is a verbal or written report to one's boss or someone higher up. Then, if the response is unsatisfactory, a complaint might be made to higher people in the organisation. Sometimes there is a board of management with representatives from outside the organisation. There often are formal internal mechanisms to deal with problems, with various names: grievance, conciliation, mediation and appeals procedures, sometimes involving trade union representatives. A professional association may have procedures to deal with breaches of professional ethics.

Then there are various government bodies. Depending on the issue, one can contact the police, the department of consumer affairs, finance department, education department, and many others. Sometimes there is an ombudsman's office or anticorruption body that deals with problems from many areas.

If there are layers of government, this expands the number of official channels. There might be local government, state or provincial government and national government, with opportunities to make complaints or formal submissions. As well as going to government bodies, it's possible to go directly to individual politicians — at any level of government — though they often refer matters to government departments. Politicians can set up further channels, such as grand juries and royal commissions.

Finally, there are courts, which can come in various types, such as small claims courts, family courts and industrial courts. Courts are also found at various levels, from local courts to a country's highest court and going beyond, for example to the International Court of Justice. Some other official channels have international analogues, notably through the United Nations.

The failure of official channels

On the face of it, there are ample opportunities to obtain justice. For those unfamiliar with the system, it seems reasonable to presume that official channels usually do their job. If there is corruption or some other injustice that can't be dealt with at a local level, then anyone with good enough documentation should be able to find officials at a higher level to fix the problem. After all, surely, that's what all these bodies and procedures were set up to do.

Unfortunately, the usual experience is just the opposite. If the problem can't be fixed up locally and informally, the official channels very seldom provide a solution. Even worse, they can chew up unbelievable amounts of money and time and provide an excuse for not dealing with the problem.

The aim of this handbook is to suggest ways to help people develop more effective strategies to achieve their goals. It is not to tell anyone what to do. It may be that using official channels is the best option in your case. But before deciding, it's worth looking at some of the evidence and arguments.

Lots of whistleblowers start out believing the system works. That's why they reported problems through official channels in the first place: they expected officials to investigate and address the problem. When, instead, they are attacked, whistleblowers often try other official channels. They still believe that the system will work — eventually. They believe that somewhere there is someone with power who will recognise the problem and implement a just solution. When one official channel fails, they try another. The process can take many years. Is it worth it?

Later on in this chapter, I tell about how to proceed through official channels if that's what you decide to do. But first I'll explain why these channels fail so often.

I'm emphasising this point because it is contrary to the instinctive response of so many people. There is a deep need to believe that the world is just. This is most obvious in Hollywood movies where the good guys always win, even against impossible odds. Filmmakers portray good triumphing over evil largely because that's what audiences want to see. Realistic stories, in which corrupt people rise to power and are never brought to justice, while the lives of honest citizens are blighted, are not welcome. Even rarer are realistic plots that show how to be an effective agent of change.

In thirty years of studying cases of suppression of dissent, and hearing hundreds of accounts of struggles through the system, I cannot remember a single example in which official channels provided a prompt and straightforward solution to a serious problem. The only cases with some degree of success through formal channels are those where there was also a process of building support, often involving publicity. On the other hand, I have heard untold numbers of harrowing stories of reprisal, victimisation and scapegoating — and the failure of official channels. Indeed, the failures of the official channels often create a sense of grievance worse than the original problem and reprisals. Although people's stories vary enormously in terms of the issue and organisation, the response of official bodies is almost always the same. Indeed, often I can predict the next development in the story.

Some people use official channels with the expectation that they will provide justice. Later, they may say "I guess I was naive." Some persist even in the face of repeated failures, or even after hearing about the evidence of other people's lack of satisfaction. They often think their case is different. After all, they know they are right. But that's not the issue. Lots of people have truth on their side, with fully documented cases, and still lose.

It is the amazing similarities of so many people's experiences that helped me reach my views about the failures of official channels. Then I talked to others with a lot of experience in this area and found they had reached identical conclusions.

One of them is Jean Lennane, a key figure in Whistleblowers Australia. A whistleblower herself, she has talked to hundreds of whistleblowers and also carried out a small survey of the responses they received from various official channels. Her conclusion is brutal. It is that you can't rely on any of the official channels. Indeed, the only thing you can rely on is that the official channels won't work.

These conclusions are based on a wealth of personal experience, but that could be a limitation. Maybe personal biases are involved. For those who prefer a more quantitative approach, Bill De Maria's research is a useful tonic. He developed a careful definition of whistleblowing and carried out a large survey of whistleblowers, asking many questions. Among them were questions about the effectiveness of various official bodies. The result: whistleblowers obtained some degree of help in less than one out of ten approaches to an official body. Even worse, in quite a few cases whistleblowers felt they were worse off after approaching official bodies. In these cases, the official channels were not just useless — they were harmful.

These results apply to whistleblowers — people who have spoken out in the public interest. Bill De Maria's results are for employees who made disclosures to a person in authority. What about the worker just doing their job who reports a safety problem or raises concerns about bias in an appointment? In many such cases, the report or concern is listened to and addressed, with no reprisals. This is business as usual, with no giant stakes or battles.

Sometimes, a person making a routine report or comment inadvertently aggravates the wrong person or puts a finger on deep corruption. Or maybe the person making the report is not satisfied with the response and persists in raising the matter. Whatever the reason, the situation goes beyond routine processes. It is at this point that an employee may decide to use a grievance procedure or make a report to a regulatory body. It is also at this point that the conclusion "the official channels seldom work" kicks in.

Lesley Pinson comments

This may seem extremely negative to the prospective whistleblower but most whistleblowers would say that had they known this at the outset, it might not have changed what they did but it would have changed their expectations and lessened the psychological impact of their experience of systems failure.

It is extremely important to be aware of the severe limitations of official channels before you try to use them.

Why official channels don't work

It helps to understand why whistleblowers so seldom find any satisfaction through official channels. If the explanation has to do with the features of particular agencies, then hope remains that other agencies might be different. But if the explanation is about all sorts of official channels, it's a different story.

Official channels always involve a narrowing of the issues. A case might involve harassment by a range of methods, for example snide and hostile comments, excessive monitoring of one's work and unrealistic expectations, followed by a disciplinary period on special conditions (set up to make the employee fail) and dismissal. When this case is taken to a grievance committee or a court, every part of the complaint or case has to be documented. Snide comments are hard to prove, and by themselves are not likely to be considered serious. Proving that one's work has been excessively monitored is difficult, because it often depends on an intimate knowledge of the job. The special conditions imposed may seem reasonable enough to an outsider who doesn't understand the realities of work. Co-workers who know what's involved may be afraid to testify. Finally, the dismissal may be completely unfair, but nevertheless proper and legal according to the letter of the employment contract.

Lesley Pinson comments

It has also been difficult, in the experience of most whistleblowers, to prove that harassment, victimisation, dismissal, etc., have occurred as a direct result of the fact that they have exposed wrongdoing. Employers use all sorts of tactics and legal machinations to directly attack the whistleblower and the whistleblower's sanity, competence, work record, etc., to divert attention from the issue exposed.

The personal experience of the victim is that there has been an injustice. Often the person targeted for such treatment is conscientious and especially committed to the official goal of the organisation. Yet the outcome of a hearing may turn on whether a person arrived slightly late to work, whether someone really raised their voice, whether the employment act permitted communicating directly to higher management, or any number of equally trivial matters. By dealing with specific actions and by arguing over the meaning of regulations and laws, the victim's experience is transformed into an administrative and technical issue. This can actually compound the feeling of injustice. Even when there is a victory, the process may not be satisfying because it has not addressed the person's whole experience. To spend weeks or months preparing a case and sit through days of hearings on technical points can be quite disempowering. A victory may be sweet partly because it's such a contrast to the bitter process.

Victories, though, are not common. A large proportion of complainants suffer the bitter process and end up losing — and are worse off than before they started. Others win comprehensively in one jurisdiction only to find that the other side appeals, requiring months or years more effort with no guarantee of ultimate success. Yet others win and return to work only to encounter new patterns of harassment and victimisation.

The next question is, why are formal channels so narrow and unsupportive of complainants? One reason is that many of these channels are set up by the organisations against which complaints are being made.

Consider a grievance procedure set up by the police, an education system, or a corporation. Almost always, those who run the procedure are senior officials. Often the complaint pits a junior person against a more senior person, or involves a challenge by a junior person against a policy approved by management.

Who will the officials side with? In just about any organisation, officials back the person with more authority. Exceptions are extremely rare. If the complaint comes from someone outside the organisation — a customer or client — the organisation is always backed against the outsider (except when the complaint is orchestrated by officials to target someone inside).

A manager may be a ruthless harasser, may be incompetent, may be corrupt, or may introduce dubious and dangerous policies. Nevertheless, higher management will almost always support such a manager against challenges from below or outside.

Sometimes this is because of personal links. The manager may have friends in high places, maybe even an entire network of mutual back-scratchers.

A deeper reason is that the system of hierarchy depends on maintaining lines of authority. If junior workers are able to win in a challenge to a manager, then what's to stop them challenging bosses higher up the ladder? Maintaining the hierarchy is crucial to managerial prerogative. All the rhetoric about efficiency and fair play goes out the window when it comes to protecting the formal system through which power is exercised.

Imagine, then, a grievance committee that decides to be independent. If it rules against senior figures, those figures would become enemies of the committee members. The committee members would come under scrutiny by top management. They might be replaced or come under attack themselves. And what about a grievance committee that rules against the chief executive officer? Who has ever heard of such an amazing event? Usually grievance committees are established to formally report to top management. In the end, they are not independent sources of power, but are subordinate to the top officials in the organisation. Usually they never think of stepping out of line. But if they do, there are powerful sanctions against an escalation of the process.

It is possible to achieve small victories through internal grievance procedures, for example in the case of blatant violations that threaten to be a public relations disaster if they are not dealt with internally. It's difficult enough to achieve small victories. But when the problem goes right to the top of the organisation or involves people with strong connections, it becomes extremely difficult to win.

Since internal appeal mechanisms are so compromised, the obvious solution is independent appeal bodies. That's the rationale for ombudsmen, anticorruption bodies, auditors-general, antidiscrimination agencies and the courts. The principle of independence is vital, but the reality is seldom so inspiring. There are several reasons why.

Sometimes appeal bodies that are nominally independent become pawns of the organisations they are supposed to police. They might be staffed with personnel who have the same values as those organisations. Often they might be former employees. For example, top management in a government consumer affairs bureau might be more sympathetic to corporations than to consumers.

In other cases, organisational self-interest is the key to the weakness of appeal bodies. To maintain funding, the body can't afford to offend too many powerful individuals. In trying to promote compliance to regulations, a softly-softly approach is taken, which to outsiders may seem like a do-nothing approach. Soon the appeal body is fatally compromised.

Other bodies retain some degree of commitment to their formal goals, but are drastically under-resourced. Complaints and requests pour in, but there simply aren't enough workers to deal with a fraction of them. A single worker may have to deal with 50 or more cases at a time. Complainants who expect a full-scale investigation into their case are usually disappointed.

Finally, in those rare cases where an independent body takes a really crusading stand, it becomes vulnerable to attack. To deal with abuses of power in a major sector of society usually means exposing a pervasive failure to act by governments and corporations. An independent body that threatens powerful groups will be smeared, have personnel changed, have its mandate changed and have its funding reduced or removed. In fact, it will be dealt with in exactly the way that whistleblowers are commonly treated.

Some scholars who analyse these things believe that appeal bodies and laws are established mainly for symbolic purposes. An anti-corruption agency or whistleblower legislation gives the public the impression that the government takes corruption seriously. Actually, these mechanisms may be set up to fail, and may fail miserably. Whistleblowers may be worse off, because they incorrectly believe that help is available, and this may delay or deter them from taking other, more effective actions.

Case study: Writing to authorities: is it worthwhile?

People write many thousands of letters to politicians and government departments about corruption, dangers to the public or whatever the correspondent is concerned about. Indeed, some individuals have written hundreds of letters on their own. Is this a worthwhile method of getting results?

Speaking to a politician face-to-face or by phone often can produce better results than a letter, though even in these cases a follow-up letter is useful. But it can be quite difficult to actually get to speak to a politician. As well, a letter has the advantage of providing a permanent record.

If you write a letter to the Prime Minister or some other minister, it is normally referred to the relevant department. It is passed down the bureaucratic hierarchy to some public servant who is assigned the responsibility of drafting a reply. The draft is then passed back up the hierarchy, sometimes being modified on the way. It is quite unusual for a minister to actually read a reply, even when his or her name appears at the bottom of the letter, which is not very often for "important" politicians. What you receive is a response from some public servant.

I talked to three public servants who gave me candid comments on how the system operates. I'll start with the most optimistic account.

Chris is a relatively new public servant who drafts replies to letters written to a leading minister. She is told by others to be as bland as possible. However, she prefers to be more conscientious. As well as finding out the other side of the story to that of the letter-writer, she sometimes will follow up the issue by ringing other departments to ensure that some action is taken. For example, if the matter falls within the jurisdiction of a state government, she will write a note or ring relevant people to make sure they respond, instead of just writing back to the letter-writer to say that the matter is one for the state government. She says that a small percentage of public servants go out of their way to help letter-writers, but most give perfunctory responses.

Chris recommends that letter-writers ask one or two specific questions. For example, "Is the minister aware of X? What are you going to do about it? I'm looking forward to your answer." Such direct questions are more difficult to wriggle out of. She also says there is lots of shuffling of letters between departments to find the right place. Therefore, you should find out beforehand exactly who you should write to. Also, send copies to other departments to make sure you are not fobbed off. (Since providing these comments to me, Chris has left the public service for a different career. She was not the right sort of person to thrive as a public servant!)

Thomas has years of experience in a major government department. He says that an individual person's complaint is normally ignored or dismissed. The department can stall by interpreting regulations differently, not responding, delaying through referral to committees, and a host of other methods. Public servants are trained in how to respond to protect current policy, in other words how to lie.

In Thomas's view, writing letters will only have an impact if the writer represents a powerful force, such as a large number of people or prestigious figures such as judges, in which case writing may not be required anyway. The other time writing can have an impact is when potentially damaging disclosures might be made unless action is taken. Such disclosures could be made to the media. According to Thomas, media coverage is detested by bureaucrats and is the best way to get action. It is a waste of time for a whistleblower just to write a letter, since the power of the whistleblower comes from publicity.

Chris notes that when it comes to potentially damaging disclosures, contacting opposition politicians is sometimes effective. They want to embarrass the government, at least on some issues, especially through asking questions in parliament.

Alan has an even more cynical view of writing letters. He believes that many letters from whistleblowers, even though sent to different departments, are referred to the same department where they are answered by the same person! This is quite possible since there are very detailed systems of numbering and tracking of letters. Thus, a whistleblower may have the illusion of contacting different authorities when actually being thwarted in the same way over and over. Alan would go even further to suggest that writing to the government provides a way for a small group of public servants to keep tabs on whistleblowers.

There are a few public servants and politicians who will do what they can for you. However, the general message from Chris, Thomas and Alan, plus others I've talked to, is that writing letters to government is largely a waste of time.

Making a decision

It's hard to give specific advice about whether certain agencies or laws are likely to be helpful, whether it is the Merit Protection Review Agency, the False Claims Act or the Anti-Corruption Commission. There are too many variables to say much reliably.

- Each country has its own set of official channels. Some countries have ombudsmen, some don't. Some have regulatory bodies for particular industries or professions, some don't.
- Different states, regions and organisations have specific official channels.

- Things change. New laws are introduced. Effective agencies become muzzled, gutted or just lose steam. Ineffective agencies are given a new lease on life. Good advice on where to go one year may be outdated the next.
- The choice of what channel to try depends sensitively on the case: what the issues are, how good the evidence is, how much you and others are willing to support it, and other factors.

Because of these variables, you need to find out for yourself about the most appropriate channel or channels for your purposes. Luckily, the general rules for doing this are straightforward.

- List possible options.
- Investigate promising options.
- Weigh up the benefits and costs of the most promising options.

The first step is to *list possible options*. There are several standard types.

- Grievance or appeal procedures internal to an organisation
- Processes run by a trade union or professional association, such as a medical complaints panel
- Government agencies, such as ombudsmen, police, antidiscrimination boards and regulatory bodies
- Courts, including specialist courts such as industrial courts
- Bodies with specific short-term briefs such as parliamentary committees and royal commissions

Just listing all the possibilities can be quite a task and may require some asking around. If you can find someone who has tried several options, that's very helpful. Sometimes ringing a staff person in one of the agencies can provide information about other options.

If you're worried about revealing your involvement in an area, do not give your name or contact details, or have a friend ring to ask what someone should do who wants to have a problem investigated.

It may seem like a lot of fuss and bother to list all these possibilities when you already know about one or two agencies that seem quite appropriate. But sometimes it's worth the trouble. Certain agencies may be very well known, but that doesn't mean they are effective. Quite possibly they are overloaded because so many people contact them. Sometimes there is a conscientious agency that only receives a few complaints each year. It might turn out to be your best bet.

> ### Cynthia Kardell comments
>
> The first step is always to educate yourself about the investigative body. Make yourself familiar with its history, role, function and processes. Know what it can and can't do, and develop a back-up plan for when it fails. Ask yourself: is your complaint one that the investigative body would be willing to spend a lot of money on? (Investigations bite into the budget!)

The next step is to *investigate promising options*. You can probably eliminate some options quickly because they don't apply to your situation. If you are confronted by financial fraud by top management, then internal organisational procedures won't be of much use, nor will antidiscrimination boards — unless the fraud has some ethnic or other element covered by antidiscrimination legislation. However, it's best not to eliminate options too quickly. Sometimes there are original ways to proceed.

Cynthia Kardell, whistleblower and long-time office bearer in Whistleblowers Australia (president since 2011).

After eliminating some options, you need to begin the real task of investigation. What do you need to find out? Here are some key things.

- What sort of documentation is required? Is it enough to mention a few incidents and let the agency investigate from there? Do you need to supply copies of documents, signed statements, names and dates, etc.?
- How much documentation is needed? Is a one-page letter enough, or will eventually hundreds of pages of submissions be required?
- How much work will be involved? Will the work required take hours, days, weeks, months or years?
- How long will it take? Will the process be over quickly (a few weeks), or will it drag on for months or years?
- What are the chances of success? Of people with cases like yours, what proportion win or get satisfaction? One out of two? One out of ten?

One approach is to look at the formal requirements. Agencies often produce guidelines telling how to make a submission. In some cases this is useful, but it seldom gives much insight into what's involved.

By far the best way to get answers is to talk to people who have been through the same processes. They can tell you all about it and give you a realistic picture.

The hard part is tracking down these people. Commonly, the names of prior complainants are confidential. If there is an action group, support group or whistleblowers group in your area, that is your best bet. For example, if your complaint is about the medical system, try to find a medical consumers group. If your complaint is about an environmental issue, contact an environmental organisation. If you are confronted by financial corruption, there may be a shareholders association.

A warning: make sure the group is genuine. Some groups with helpful-sounding names are actually industry front groups or defend professionals against clients. For example, many polluting industries fund bogus "citizen" groups to campaign on their behalf. How can you tell the difference? Personal contacts are a good way. Also, you can ask the groups for names of clients who are willing to talk about their experiences. (Even this can be faked!)

If there is no obvious group or individual to give you first-hand advice, then your task is more difficult. Sometimes there are official statistics about the outcomes of cases. However, these can be misleading. A large proportion of cases, whether in internal organisation procedures or in the courts, are settled before they go through all the formal stages. You might be able to find records of court decisions, but that won't give you information about cases settled out of court.

Try to find a knowledgeable insider who will give you the lowdown on what actually happens. In most organisations there is at least one individual who knows a lot about the organisation's problems and how they have been dealt with. If you can find one or two such individuals and tap into their reservoirs of knowledge, the insights you gain will be invaluable. They may know about people who tried to change the system, and know what happened to them.

Robina Cosser comments

People are not always what they seem to be, so seeking a knowledgeable insider may put you at risk. Sometimes it's safer to collect evidence and not speak to anyone.

There are such people everywhere, but in most cases you have to be an insider yourself to gain access to them. For example, in any agency there will be people who can give an honest appraisal of what has worked and what hasn't. This information will greatly help you in deciding how best to proceed and how to avoid traps that snared others before you. The best way to track these people down is through friendship networks.

Doing a thorough investigation of options can be very time-consuming and frustrating. If you can recruit some friends or supporters — especially those with good connections — it can be much easier. The bigger the issue, the more careful your investigation should be. Think of it this way.

- If you find out that certain channels are not worth trying, that may save you thousands of dollars and months of work.
- If you learn a few tips about how to make your case more effective, that may make the difference between success and failure.

Chapter 5 emphasised the importance of collecting plenty of documentation, more than most people ever imagined was necessary. The same applies to investigating options: you should investigate more than you ever imagined was necessary.

If you are involved in sports, you know that preparation is the key to success. This includes training, mental and physical. It includes studying the rules. It includes finding out about opponents.

Making a formal submission is like playing a game. You need to have prepared exceptionally well, to know your opponent and to know the best way to play. The other side probably has lots more money and resources to use against you. To have a chance of winning, you need every advantage possible. Being clever helps!

Another source of information is books, journals and the internet. Contact your librarian or a friendly researcher to help you find out about options. Perhaps someone has written an article or a thesis about the agency or about the fate of certain types of complaints. News stories can be helpful too. You can use computer databases to track down articles, court reports and much else. If you can find a useful study or commentary about the path you're planning, that's useful in itself. If you have more questions, perhaps you can contact the author.

There are some other sources of information about which you need to be wary:

- Senior people in the organisation. You are unlikely to obtain a realistic picture from them.
- Agency workers. They may tell you the official line, which is invariably optimistic and sometimes damaging. Sometimes you may get quite helpful advice. The challenge is to know which is which.
- Lawyers. They are unlikely to give you an honest account of the disadvantages of legal action, including great expense and long time delays. A few are corrupt.

Who should you trust? You should be wary of those who have some stake in a particular process or outcome, such as officials and lawyers. You can have more trust in those who have nothing to gain by your choice, such as librarians or researchers. You can put most trust in those who have confronted the same sort of problems that you have and who have made sacrifices in their pursuit of justice.

Cynthia Kardell comments

It's best to start by trusting, but if you trust anyone or any process, be alert for the first indication that all might not be well. Trust your instincts. If needed, protect yourself and take a different tack.

(There can always be exceptions. Some lawyers and agency officials are pushing for change and can be your best allies. Some researchers are far from independent, being financially or ideologically in the back pocket of your opponents.)

Finally, if your information is limited, here are some rules of thumb, based on the experience of whistleblowers.

- Estimate how much of your money and effort the process should take if it was handled sensibly by all parties. Then multiply by 10 or 100 to get an estimate of the actual amounts. If you estimate a week's work (40 hours), then the actual figure could easily be several months or even years.
- Estimate how long the process should take if it was run efficiently. Then multiply by 10 to get an estimate how long it will take. If it should be over in six months, the actual time could be five years.
- Estimate the chance of success if everything was fair. Then divide by 10 to get an estimate of your actual chance of success. If you think your chance should be 50% (1 out of 2), then your actual chance is probably closer to 5% (1 out of 20).

This may seem terribly pessimistic. Although the numerical procedures are arbitrary, the general approach is right. Most people challenging the system greatly underestimate how much money, effort and time will be required and greatly overestimate their chances of success. These rules of thumb are designed to bring some realism into the process.

Now it's time to *weigh up the benefits and costs of the most promising options*. This is a process that involves what you've found out about the options, plus your own values and goals.

One useful technique is to write down two lists: benefits and costs. This helps to clarify what's involved. The decision may not be any easier, but you are less likely to miss some important point. Here are two general lists that cover many typical benefits and costs.

Benefits	*Costs*
Expose problem	Diversion from problem
Prevent continuation of problem	Time
Set an example/precedent	Expense
Compensation	Trauma
Improved work situation	Worse work situation
Self-respect	Discrediting
Vindication	Diversion from other options

The first three benefits are mostly for the organisation or society rather than you personally. By taking an issue to an official channel, you may help expose the problem. This is especially true if you link your appeal with a publicity campaign, as described in the next chapter. Also, your action may help prevent the problem continuing, by alerting authorities or by putting the organisation on notice. Your case may even set an example that others can follow or set a precedent for employees or citizens to take similar action.

Then there are benefits to you personally. Compensation might be a monetary pay-out or retirement package. An improved work situation might be a return to the status quo before you spoke out, a reduction in attacks, or a change in location or boss. If you lost your job, a return to work can be a major benefit.

Finally, there are benefits that are primarily psychological. Pursuing a case can give self-respect, regardless of what happens along the way, because it means you have taken a stand against injustice and persevered against great odds. If the case is successful, this can vindicate your stand. Even if you lose, you may feel better than doing nothing and later feeling guilty when the problem continues and claims further victims.

Lesley Pinson comments

I felt overwhelmingly that if I didn't do as much as I could and there was a serious accident, I would forever feel dreadful that I hadn't done anything. Also, I feared that if I didn't report corruption and it was subsequently exposed, then I would look foolish or be found professionally negligent if I was ever asked "But you knew about this, why didn't you report it?"

What about motivations that we usually don't admit — such as revenge? Well, that's up to you. This book is about being effective, not getting even.

Now for the costs of using official channels. Although in the best scenario, dealing with your case through official channels may bring attention to the problem, in the worst scenario it may do the opposite: divert attention from the problem by dealing with all sorts of minor irrelevant issues.

Major costs are time and expense, as discussed earlier. Months of work and large costs are common. Perhaps you will put your life savings at risk. Another major cost is trauma. This includes reopening discussion of topics that previously disturbed you as well as the mounting of new attacks. If you still have your job, the case may make your situation worse by opening you to harassment.

It's important to remember that you may end up with official decisions made against you. This could serve to discredit you and the causes you support. Finally, pursuing official channels may divert you from other options. All the time and money you spend on the case might have been devoted to some other course of action. This is the "opportunity cost" of this path.

So — you've written down the benefits and costs. How do you make a decision? This isn't easy. One of the most difficult parts is that you don't know what will happen. This isn't like buying a house where you know, pretty much, what you will get. It's more like taking a huge gamble.

To start, it can help to separate out the certain consequences from the ones that depend on the outcome. You can list things you think are sure to happen as definite, those more likely to happen than not as probable and those less likely than this as possible. The lists might look like this.

Definite benefit	*Definite costs*
Self-respect	Time
	Expense
	Diversion from other options
Probable benefit	*Probable costs*
Expose problem	Trauma
	Diversion from problem
Possible benefits	*Possible costs*
Prevent continuation of problem	Worse work situation
Set an example/precedent	Discrediting
Compensation	
Improved work situation	
Vindication	

Whereas the original list just gave all outcomes without any assessment, this listing is a move towards what is likely. To refine this a bit, it can be useful to eliminate items that aren't so important to you, leaving just the ones that are crucial. For example, let's say that the financial side is vital, because you have a family to support. You have plenty of time — after you lost your job! On the psychological side, self-respect is very important, but you are worried about reopening the wounds. The list of essentials boils down to this.

Definite benefit   *Definite cost*
Self-respect   Expense

Possible benefit   *Probable cost*
Compensation   Trauma

Even with this shorter list, the comparisons can be difficult. Let's say you expect the expense to be $50,000, including legal costs and income forgone, and the likely compensation if you win to be $250,000. Then, this is a fair wager if your chance of success is one in five. Are you a gambler? Would you bet $50,000 on a horse at 4-1 odds?

Comparing the financial benefits and costs is the easy part! How can you compare maintaining self-respect with a likelihood of continued trauma? What if other people — your family — are affected too? There are no easy answers.

There's one sure thing, though. You are more likely to make a sensible decision by laying out the options and consequences and thinking them through than by acting in the heat of the moment. Emotions are always involved, to be sure. But when it comes to making a decision, it helps to have thought through the options.

There are several important points to keep in mind when making a decision.

Success is rare. Most people tend to overestimate their chance of success using official channels. Let's say that you've worked out that the chance of winning through this particular appeal procedure is less than one out of ten, because you've heard of only one definite victory and know at least ten complainants who lost or gave up along the way. Nevertheless, many people tend to discount the figures because they know, deep in their hearts, that their own case is really good. How could it lose, with rock-solid documentation? This is the time to remember that success through official channels is not about being right but about winning against the other side's tactics.

Another factor is that most people are not good at integrating probabilities in decision making. The chance of winning may be one in ten, but in comparing benefits and costs it is tempting to think of them on equal terms.

The key is to compare options. You've summed up the benefits and costs of this option. Now you need to do the same with other options. This is a way of finding the option that has the best balance of benefits and costs. You might decide that you would go ahead on option A, because by your assessment the benefits outweigh the costs. But it's worth checking options B and C too, because they might be even better. Furthermore, you may find that you can proceed with options A *and* B at the same time, improving your odds.

Check with others. Be sure to consult with others, especially those closest to you and those who know most about the options. They may be able to warn you if you are making unrealistic assumptions or if you've forgotten some important factors. Ultimately, though, the decision is yours.

An extra reminder on overestimating success

There are several common psychological factors that make people overestimate their chance of success — and to gamble when the odds are very bad.

First, most people are overconfident about their own abilities. For example:

- 90% of workers said they are more productive than the median worker;

- 70% of final-year high school students said they had more leadership ability than average;
- 60% of these students said they were in the top 10% in their ability to get along with others;
- 94% of academics said they were better at their jobs than an average colleague.[1]

Second, success is highly salient compared to failure. Those who lose or give up along the way are usually less prominent. We hear a lot about lottery winners but seldom about the many losers. We hear a lot about a few famous basketball or soccer players but never about the many kids who waste years unsuccessfully trying to make the big time. Similarly, if someone wins a major court case against a corrupt boss, it is likely to be reported in the media and become an example. Losers seldom make the news.

Third, people tend to throw good money after bad. Psychologically, there's a tendency to try to recoup money lost in an investment by putting in more money. Similarly, someone who has spent weeks of work and waited a year to have a complaint heard is strongly tempted to keep trying even though the return may not be worth the trouble.

Fourth, many people believe that, after a string of heads when flipping a coin, tails is more likely. Actually, the odds are the same. After trying a series of appeal channels and being repeatedly unsuccessful, some may think they've had a string of bad luck and that the next attempt is bound to be more successful. Wrong. If anything, it's less likely to succeed since the more promising avenues were tried at the beginning.

---

[1] Robert H. Frank and Philip J. Cook, *The Winner-Take-All Society: Why the Few at the Top Get So Much More Than the Rest of Us* (New York: Penguin, 1996), p. 104.

So — your case is rock-solid and you know that you are in the right. Other people may lose cases but yours is different. Think again! Other people also had rock-solid cases and were in the right — but they lost. The other side used legal loopholes, nasty tricks, obfuscation and delays, keeping the cases going for years. Victory can be both rare and expensive even when official channels are fair. When officials are corrupt, your task is even more difficult.

Some degree of overconfidence can be useful, otherwise we would never try or risk anything. But it's vital to be as realistic as possible when comparing options. All options need to be examined in terms of benefits and costs, not just the size of the glittering prize at the end. All options are risky. All the more reason to pick the one with the best prospects.

Staying the distance

You've made your decision: you're going ahead with it. You've begun the process: a grievance mechanism, a complaint to an agency, a court case. Soon you'll know more about procedures than you ever thought necessary. If you're going to use this channel, it makes sense to use it well.

Learn everything you can about the process. It makes sense to follow the required specifications as closely as possible, unless you have some principled objection. If you have to make a submission, write it well and follow the standard format.

Contact, if you can, people who have been through the process already, especially those who found it satisfactory. Listen to their advice carefully. Look at their documents. Is your own case missing something? Ask them what they found to be the weakest point in their case, and then work on making your own case as strong as possible in that area.

Make sure you know how many procedures and appearances you could have to go through, assuming the other side appeals to higher jurisdictions. Otherwise, it may be halfway through your first case when you find out what you're in for.

Dress for success. If you need to appear in person, try to figure out what sorts of clothes and grooming will make the best impression. Appear respectable and serious, without overdoing it. Some agencies are more formal than others.

Practise to improve your performance. If you have to make a written submission, write draft after draft, getting comments on how to improve it from anyone with knowledge and experience.

If you have to speak or answer questions, do some practice sessions. Prepare your talk carefully and then practise it by yourself in front of a mirror. You can refer to brief notes or cue cards, but never read a talk. Practise it over and over until your nerves are reduced to a tolerable level. Better yet, get a tape recorder and listen to your talk. Then revise the talk, and your style, step by step. Focus on improving just one aspect at a time.

Next, get a friend to be an audience, and give your talk. If you're still very nervous, try it again — and again. Get feedback from your friend on how to improve, both content and delivery. No one becomes a brilliant speaker overnight, but it is possible to improve considerably by preparation and practice. You may never eliminate nervousness, but it is possible to keep it under control.

If you have to answer questions, practice is again crucial. Write down the questions you think are the most difficult. Work out your best possible answers and then practise them. Give the questions to a friend and have the friend ask you the questions and listen to your answers. Then get your friend to make up new questions and ask you to answer without preparation. Ask people who've been through the process before what sort of questions come up. Get advice about what sorts of answers are most effective. Answering questions is a skill that can be improved by preparation and practice.

Cynthia Kardell comments

If there are things you are uncertain or embarrassed about or things you know others will try to blame you for, talk it through with a trusted confidant beforehand and get used to answering difficult questions in a thoughtful, quietly confident way. If you learn how to respond to delicate questions and be safe, the other side won't be able to undermine you.

The same applies to your emotions. If you sometimes lose your temper or become visibly upset, your opponents may be tempted to take advantage of your emotional vulnerability, either by planning in advance or operating instinctively on the spur of the moment. Think of the sorts of comments or situations that trigger an emotional response that may weaken your case. Plan a method of response that keeps you in control, for example a behaviour ("pause and take three deep breaths before responding") or a set of ideas or images ("a calm, crisp reply"). Practise your plan by yourself and then with a friend.

Advocates

Choose your advocates carefully. If you are represented by an advocate, for example by a lawyer in a court case, choose carefully — assuming you have a choice. Consult with others to find out about their experiences. If someone who has been through the same process recommends an advocate, that is a good endorsement. Sometimes you can find out about the advocate by looking up court records or other files. Don't hesitate to do so. If you're spending lots of money and time on the case, it makes sense to investigate thoroughly to ensure that you have the best possible advocate.

Try to find someone who is oriented to results rather than process. The results-oriented advocate is willing to push things forward in order to get what you want most out of the process, whether it's an apology, a pay-out or a precedent-setting judgement. The process-oriented advocate, on the other hand, tends to respond to the requirements of the system, going through a standard procedure, allowing the maximum time or waiting for the other side to take an initiative. This often increases your costs while delaying things.

Your advocate should be willing to follow your instructions. The advocate may know a lot more about the system than you do, so you should consider the advocate's advice carefully. But you know more about your case than anyone. If you've also learned a lot about the process, you may wish to overrule your advocate's recommendation. Go ahead. It's your choice.

Lesley Pinson comments

You should also listen to and act on your instincts. Psychologically, when you act against your better judgement and instincts because of the advice of others, then if this advice proves to be wrong it leads to a lot of bitterness and anger against your advocate which is a diversion from the main game. (Quite a few whistleblowers end up taking action against their own lawyers.) You end up bitterly regretting that you didn't do what you believed was right in the first place.

Much better is to listen to your instincts and do what you believe is right. If that proves to be wrong, it is a hell of a lot easier to move on and live with your own mistakes.

Whistleblowers tend to put far too much faith in their legal advocates. This is doomed. It is important to keep your advocates on their toes. It is dangerous to sit back and rest comfortably with the expectation that someone else is now going to solve things for you. This is when things can go very badly wrong. You must always retain control over your case and be responsible for it.

Jean Lennane comments

It's possible to use the legal system effectively, but quite a lot of insight and skill is required. For example, it's worthwhile aiming to achieve a series of small legal wins in order to end up where you want to go.

Unfortunately, 95% of lawyers are a waste of time or worse for whistleblowers. The cases simply aren't rewarding enough for lawyers to do a good job.

Whistleblowers sometimes qualify as lawyers in order to handle their own cases. If your case is likely to last five years or more — and many do — then qualifying is worth it. More specialist lawyers are needed to help whistleblowers.

Change your advocate if necessary. If you're unhappy with the support or advice you've been receiving, go ahead and change. It could be that your advocate is overloaded, has personal problems, isn't interested, isn't competent or is corrupt. An incompetent advocate may lose the case by making mistakes in procedure, using the wrong arguments or just presenting the arguments poorly. A corrupt advocate could be paid off by the other side, hope for some benefit by not rocking the boat, or have friends in high places.

It's better to change than to persist with someone you don't trust or who isn't giving satisfactory service. However, just because you lost the case doesn't mean your advocate was incompetent or corrupt. The other side might have had more talented advocates hired at huge expense.

Cynthia Kardell comments

If you decide to change your advocate, do it early, before things get nasty, because you don't need another fight on your hands. Get another advocate lined up. Don't openly criticise your former advocate. Let the new advocate tell the former one about the change. If you need to sue the former advocate down the track, you can.

Obtain independent advice. Talk to people who have nothing to gain or lose from the outcome of your case. See what they think. What is the best next step? Are you being too demanding of your advocate? Is it appropriate to compromise?

Independent advice is vital because you can trust it more. A paid advocate may well have developed a standard procedure that tends to increase the length of the case — and the advocate's pay. A union official is likely to put union interests — or personal career interests — higher than your case. This is natural enough and need not involve conscious scheming or corruption.

Reassess your strategy regularly. As the case progresses, the situation changes. Your finances or your personal relationships may be different. Your goals may change. There may be facts revealed that change your perspective about the situation. So go back to the drawing board and look at your strategy (see chapter 4). Is it time to call it quits? Is it time for a dramatic new initiative? Is the present course about right?

Beware the silencing clause

Things are looking good. Your case looks like winning, or perhaps you've just won. The other side comes to you offering a settlement — usually a large amount of money. It is bound to be tempting. The money can help pay off mounting bills. Also, it means no more court appearances. After all, the other side could appeal your victory, even if they have little prospect of success, in an attempt to wear you down through years of additional litigation.

There are two catches. First, you don't obtain a formal victory. Second, and more deadly, is the silencing clause. You are expected, as part of the settlement, to sign a statement saying that you won't reveal anything about the case or even the amount of the settlement itself.

There are lots of variations on the silencing clause. The basic aim is to shut you up and prevent your case becoming a precedent for others. The other side avoids admitting liability.

The settlement is attractive, but the silencing clause is not. But often the other side will insist: no clause, no settlement.

You have to make your own decision, and your personal circumstances may virtually dictate acquiescence. Here are a few implications.

- At the beginning of litigation, be aware of the possibility of silencing agreements.
- Be prepared for options just prior to going to court.
- Be flexible, because you might change your mind if the silencing clause suppresses basic issues at stake. After all, speaking out in the public interest is a matter of making information generally available, not covering it up.
- If you are able, resist as much of any silencing clause as possible. Speaking out about the issues is more important than naming the payment you received.
- Join campaigns to ban silencing agreements.

Cynthia Kardell comments

Do not sign if everything inside you is screaming that you're being treated badly, because you'll hate yourself if you sign. Just accept that the lawyer's interest may not be yours and get out of there until you've had time to talk it over with a trusted confidant.

Appendix: Formal mediation, a semi-official channel

If you are having a conflict with someone that you can't easily sort out just between the two of you, then formal mediation may be helpful. (The term "mediation" may be used to describe different processes. This description is one example.) A neutral mediator is chosen, agreeable to both parties. The mediator meets with the two people in conflict and allows them to present and discuss their perspectives. Various outcomes are possible. Ideally, differences are resolved. More commonly, the parties recognise that their differences persist but agree to behave civilly in future. When the process is unsuccessful, one or both parties may decide to pursue their grievance in some other way.

The great advantage of mediation is that it allows people in dispute to lay their perspectives on the table in front of a neutral party. Often, this process cools tempers and improves relationships. It can open up communication channels and prevent a situation from escalating to far more damaging and irretrievable steps.

The role of the mediator is crucial. Mediators have considerable latitude. They might decide to meet each person separately before holding a joint meeting, to have a series of meetings or to run "shuttle diplomacy." They decide how to conduct meetings and need to monitor the conversation sensitively. If the mediator is not seen as neutral, this undermines the process. The mediator should not be in a position of power over any participant.

Mediation, as described here, requires a fair bit of trust. Parties participate voluntarily on their own, without advocates. Usually no formal notes are taken and there is no formal report to any organisation such as an employer. Agreements are not formally binding. Mediation does not seek "the truth" as in a formal investigation or to reach a definitive ruling as in an arbitration or court proceeding, but rather to help people to get along better.

Mediation is frequently carried out in an informal fashion in day-to-day interactions, such as when someone tries to help friends or family members to get along better, or when a co-worker swiftly intervenes to hose down a heated exchange. Some people in groups habitually take on the role of informal mediator, acting sensitively and unobtrusively to prevent things getting out of hand. Formal mediation is an attempt to build on the best aspects of this important everyday process.

For all its advantages, mediation is not always a good idea. If you are being targeted, mediation can serve as a means of attack. The biggest risk is that the mediator is not neutral, in which case meetings may be used to blame or humiliate you. Another danger is that information provided in a meeting may not be kept confidential. In the worst scenario, everything you say is fed by the mediator back to your boss or antagonist. Finally, after making a verbal agreement during mediation, there is no guarantee that the other party will hold to it.

Workplace mediation works best between co-workers who are in roughly comparable sorts of positions and who have a long-term interest in getting along. It is not so well suited for harmonising relations between boss and employee.

If you have reason to believe that a particular mediator is biased or untrustworthy, request a different mediator. If you don't fully trust the other party, don't say anything that could open you to attack. If appropriate, ask for an agreement — such as not to discuss a particular incident any more — to be put in writing and signed by both of you. Finally, if you can't see any benefits from mediation, don't participate.

Sometimes, during a legal battle, the court will offer mediation as a possible means of resolution. Make sure that you have as many people on your side as there are on the other side. It's also advisable to specify how long the process will last. If you're stuck in a room for many hours under enormous pressure to reach an agreement, the risk of making unwise concessions increases as time goes on and your energy flags.

When tempers flare, threats are made and a relationship becomes seriously soured, mediation can really help. But it's not a cure-all, and it can be abused. If you're not sure whether mediation is a good idea, discuss the possibility with friends and see whether you can talk to others who have had the same mediator.

If your problem is mainly a personal conflict, mediation can be quite helpful. But if the problem involves much more than interpersonal relations, such as serious corruption, mediation will be inadequate or even harmful.

8 Leaking

- Revealing problems while remaining anonymous has important advantages: it reduces the risk of reprisals and allows you to remain in the job and continue to collect and reveal information.
- In many situations, leaking is not suitable.
- Leaking effectively requires knowledge and skills, including how to remain anonymous, how to choose recipients for disclosures, how to communicate information and who to tell what you're doing.

Most whistleblowers are open about who they are and what they are saying. They report a problem to the boss or make a complaint to an agency or contact the media. Because they are open, they often become targets for reprisals.

Another option is to reveal problems without revealing your identity. This means you are anonymous. Your boss and your co-workers may know or believe that someone has revealed information to outsiders — but they don't know it's you.

> *Alana worked for an insurance company and discovered documents showing that top managers were changing the policies for customers living in risky areas without clearly informing them. She saved copies of these documents, electronically cleaned them of identifying information and, from a cybercafe across town, sent them to a citizens' group concerned about insurance company abuses.*

Leaking is the unauthorised disclosure of information without revealing one's identity to authorities or wider audiences. It is one method for trying to expose problems: it is a way to blow the whistle anonymously.

Leaking can also be used for other purposes. Politicians and senior government officials regularly leak information to journalists for political or personal gain. Some leaks are intended to harm others. This isn't whistleblowing.

The focus in this handbook is on whistleblowing, which includes leaking to address wrongdoing and similar problems. This might be called public interest leaking. WikiLeaks calls it "principled leaking." Public interest leaking is just like public whistleblowing, except the whistleblower seeks to do it covertly or anonymously.

Advantages of leaking

The risk of reprisals to whistleblowers is significant: their identity is known, hence they can be easily targeted. Leaking reduces these risks, sometimes greatly reduces them. The main risk is that you will be tracked down as the leaker. The better you are able to avoid detection, the greater the advantage of leaking.

Daniel Ellsberg, who in 1971 leaked the Pentagon Papers, a study of US government decision-making during the Vietnam War.

Another major advantage of leaking is that you remain in the job and can collect more information and, if appropriate, leak again to reveal problems. If you speak out and bosses know who you are, they will make sure your access to damaging information is cut off. If bosses don't know it's you, you may continue to have access and be able to leak on future occasions. You might even be put in charge of finding the leaker!

An open whistleblower often has just one chance to expose a problem. After that it is downhill, with reprisals and exclusion from sensitive information. An anonymous whistleblower can have many opportunities to expose a problem. This means the chance of making a difference is much greater. Furthermore, with leaks the attention is more on the issue and less on the person who disclosed information.

These are very big advantages. If you're thinking of speaking out about a problem, you should carefully consider whether it's possible to do so without revealing your identity.

Cynthia Kardell comments

Leaking is often seen as being a bit sneaky, not being upfront and honest. Ignore all that, as it is usually the sort of thing your detractors say to undermine and pull you down. Why make yourself a target when you don't need to?

Anonymous leaking is better than making a confidential disclosure to an investigative body, because it removes the temptation for the investigative body to cast you as the villain.

Leaking is entirely sensible and reasonable, particularly on politically sensitive issues, because all the protections promised

Leakers

WikiLeaks

by legislation and investigative bodies are only ever useful after you've suffered reprisals.

When leaking is not suitable

If you've already spoken out, it's too late to be anonymous. (However, your co-workers could leak — and blame it on you. If that's okay with you, encourage them. If not, then make sure you have convincing evidence that you're not the leaker.)

If you're easily identifiable, then trying to be anonymous may be futile. Maybe you're the only person, aside from the boss, with access to particular documents or information. Maybe the key documents are things you personally compiled or wrote. (However, you could "accidentally" leave them around for someone else to obtain and then leak.) Maybe the workplace is so small that you can't hide. Maybe you have the reputation as the person to be blamed for any exposure.

If you are easily identifiable, it may be better to be open in speaking out, thereby giving your statements more credibility, for example if you obtain media coverage.

Sometimes you don't need to be anonymous. If you've resigned, found another job, written articles and a book, and are speaking with politicians and regulators, then anonymity is unnecessary, maybe even pointless.

Sometimes you need to interact with the recipient of your leaks. You might leak some documents, but those who receive them often want to know more, for example additional evidence, how credible you are, and where the evidence comes from. They may need more information before taking action, or use your anonymity as a pretext to avoid doing anything.

Good investigative agencies, including some media, can set up secure and anonymous communication channels so you can interact with them without revealing your identity. However, the more you interact, the more likely someone will figure out who you are. You might start off being anonymous but end up being known to some people. Think through what might happen to your disclosures and be prepared.

Sometimes leaking puts you or others in danger. In some high-risk situations, for example relating to organised crime or some police and military cases, leaking may increase danger. If criminals are involved, they may take reprisals against whoever they think might be the leaker: you and others might be targeted. In such circumstances, leaking can be risky. Curiously, revealing your identity can give greater safety, because if there are serious reprisals — you are assaulted, for example — then others will know who did it and why.

If you are anonymous, you can be assaulted without as much public concern, which makes it more likely.

For this reason, witness protection schemes run by police sometimes are better avoided. The idea is good: hide and protect the witness — someone who has seen a crime — so they can't be assaulted, threatened or otherwise prevented from giving testimony. The trouble is that the police running the witness protection scheme may have links with criminals, and you could be at greater risk. If you are open about your identity and location, attackers will know that anything they do will be widely publicised.

In high-risk situations, it's vital to carefully consider options, including not revealing anything. If you're going to leak information, try to assess the ramifications and figure out the best time and methods. This applies to any leaking, but is even more important when lives are at stake.

Who can receive leaks

WikiLeaks has provided massive media attention to leaking, but leaking has occurred for a long time. There are two traditional recipients of leaks and two newer ones.

Journalists

Scenario 1. An employee collects a parcel of damning documents, sticks them into an envelope and posts them to a journalist. The journalist explores further, writes a story and the issue is exposed. These days, sending documents by email is more common.

Scenario 2. An employee rings a journalist and reveals damning information. The journalist explores further, writes a story and the

Wikileekz cat iz in ur dokumentz...

leekin'...

issue is exposed. The employee might meet the journalist face-to-face, mainly use a phone, or prefer texting and email.

The main difference between these two scenarios is whether the journalist knows the leaker's identity. Scenario 1 maintains the greatest anonymity for the leaker. In scenario 2, the journalist knows who the leaker is, so the leaker needs to trust the journalist.

Can a journalist be trusted with maintaining your identity? This is a matter of judgement. Most journalists are trustworthy, and some have gone to prison rather than reveal the identity of informants.

In most cases, a more important question is, will a journalist take your material seriously and do a good story? If your material is old, unexciting or incomprehensible, few journalists will be interested. If your material is current, deals with a hot topic, and is nicely organised (perhaps with a summary and time line you've carefully written), then a good journalist should be able to turn it into a story. Possible obstacles include reluctant editors, conflicts of interest, sheer overload (journalists often have inadequate time to do investigative stories), inexperience and incompetence.

Look at a journalist's previous work. If a journalist has a track record of breaking important stories, this is a good sign. However, there are no guarantees.

Activist groups

Environmental groups, residents' groups, anti-corruption groups, political parties, unions — these are some of the groups that might receive leaks. If key activists are interested in your material, they might publicise it through their own networks or arrange for various forms of media coverage.

Which group? It depends on what you're revealing.

- Environmental problems: an environmental group, obviously enough
- Corruption in local government: a residents' group
- Political corruption: an honesty-in-politics group or perhaps a political party on the other side (be careful: both sides might be involved in the corruption)

Why go to an activist group rather than a journalist? Usually the reason is that the group — or a particular member — has a special interest in the topic and will be willing to put time and energy into making best use of it. A story on television might be seen by lots of viewers, but few of them will do anything about it, whereas a story in a group's newsletter might stimulate a campaign.

If you find a receptive group, an initial leak could be the beginning of an ongoing relationship, which might be more productive than dealing with journalists, for whom producing a story is of prime importance. Activists may not need documents or even special information: insight into how your organisation operates can be valuable and enable more effective campaigning.

How should you decide whether a group is a suitable recipient? If the group has a track record of revealing inside information in a responsible, effective way, this is a good sign. Often there are just one or two people in the group with experience and initiative to make good use of leaks. Making contact with experienced, responsible, strategically sophisticated individuals is advisable. Newcomers with energy and enthusiasm might promise a lot but not deliver, or even inadvertently compromise your situation through carelessness or over-eagerness.

Some groups are overloaded — indeed, most activist groups are overloaded. The problems are bigger than what they have the time and energy to deal with. So your material might get lost in a deluge of incoming issues. Some groups have paid staff, who are likely to be highly knowledgeable but also overloaded. Sometimes a volunteer is a better bet.

Few activist groups have much experience with leakers. They might need time to learn.

The combination of concerned insiders (the leakers) with committed outsiders (the activists) can be extremely powerful. The insiders can alert the activists to abuses, plans and internal thinking, and can suggest the sorts of questions or actions that would be most effective, for example drafting articles, media releases, freedom of information requests or questions to ask in parliament. The activists can tell the insiders what sorts of issues are most important and what sorts of information would be most useful.

WikiLeaks and other online operations

WikiLeaks was the first online system for leaking. Using it is very much like posting or emailing documents to a journalist or activist, except that documents are uploaded to a website. WikiLeaks staff decide whether the material is worth publishing. If so, there are two main options. One is that the material is directly posted online. The other is that the material is first made available to selected media outlets before being posted online.

WikiLeaks thus is analogous to a publishing operation, combining the roles of journalist, editor and publisher. It plays the role of journalist in telling a story about the leaked material, though this may involve only a brief introduction to the documents. It plays the role of editor in deciding what should be published and in what form. It plays the role of publisher by posting the documents online.

The success of WikiLeaks in obtaining and releasing highly contentious material, and coming under attack, especially by the US government, has led to the development of other online leaking operations, and it is likely that more will emerge in the future.

Online leaking has several advantages. The main one is that publication of documents occurs online. This gives ongoing visibility worldwide.

WikiLeaks has shown courage in publishing material that national media outlets would not, because of likely reprisals. Conventional publishers and activist groups have established identities and can be held accountable for their actions. In contrast, most of the members of WikiLeaks are unknown to the public. Julian Assange has become highly visible, giving the misleading impression that he is solely responsible for the group's activities. There are many others behind the scenes, ensuring that the systems operate.

Anonymity of the publisher adds an extra degree of independence to WikiLeaks compared to conventional publishers. This suggests that WikiLeaks is especially worth considering for extremely high-impact disclosures, for example when reprisals might involve physical threats. Publicity about release of US diplomatic cables has overshadowed other WikiLeaks exposes, for example about corruption in African countries.

WikiLeaks also has some disadvantages. It is seldom possible to personally discuss documents as you would with a journalist or activist — there is no one to help you compose a persuasive story. To be effective using WikiLeaks, documents need to tell their own story, or be sufficiently interesting to regular journalists so that they will write stories about them.

Cynthia Kardell comments

If WikiLeaks decides to post your material, you could — if sufficiently savvy — start blogging or twittering anonymously or posting bits on YouTube and bringing it to the attention of online activist groups.

Direct to the public

If you want, you can leak direct to your desired audience, without relying on anyone else.

In the years before the Internet, Stephen produced a newsletter for his colleagues at work. It was anonymous and unauthorised,

> *and exposed problems in a humorous way. He collected information, wrote little stories and produced a newsletter every couple of months. He did the printing and photocopying at another location. After hours, he put copies in the mailboxes of workers — including his own, to reduce suspicion. His bosses never figured out who was doing it.*

With the Internet, leaking directly is fairly easy. The basic idea is to make copies of documents, or write your own analysis of the situation, and make this available to your audience. One method is to email copies to particular individuals, expecting that they will forward the email to others. Another prime method is to post the material on a website — and then email some people to alert them to the web address.

To maintain anonymity, precautions are needed. You can set up a new email account and put documents on an anonymous site. You may need to do all this from a computer far from your home, that cannot be linked to you.

The advantage of direct leaking is that you don't need anyone else's help to get the information out (unless you need technical assistance). You can control the way the material and the message are presented. The disadvantage is that you may miss out on the added visibility that can come from involving journalists, activists or online leaking operations.

Remaining anonymous, being effective

Bosses and authorities will go to amazing lengths to find out who is leaking information. Maintaining anonymity can be a major challenge. So it's vital to plan ahead, thinking about what others might to do track you down and expose you, and making sure they won't succeed.

The techniques for leaking change with time, especially as new technologies become available, both for leaking and for controlling information and tracking down leakers. Therefore, rather than providing a detailed prescription for leaking, it's more useful to list the general areas to be aware of.

Documents

You have a document and send it to an online site. Safe enough? Maybe not. For example, Microsoft Word documents, under "Properties," list the author and the computer where it is stored. Before passing such documents to others, you need to clean the file of any information that might indicate your involvement.

Some employers will change the text in documents, in minor, inconspicuous ways, for each of the recipients. Therefore, if the document is published online, the employer might be able to determine that it was the copy given to you or someone else. Even more subtly, an electronic document may contain an invisible signature that tells when it was produced and perhaps which copy it is.

How careful to be depends on how paranoid the bosses are. It is safer to be extra careful. To get rid of electronic signatures, for example, you might photocopy the document and then scan the photocopied image. But be sure to use a photocopier away from the workplace, because some photocopiers leave traces that can be used to help track you down.

Computers and messages

If you write up an account of things that have been happening, it's very risky to do it on your work computer. Your boss, or computer specialists hired by your boss, might go into your computer and access the files. Don't use your work computer for emails about leaked documents either: they can be accessed.

So what about your home computer, or your phone, or some other device? These are safer, but if you really want to be secure, then think ahead to the worst scenario. Suppose someone breaks into your home and steals your computer or your phone. They can get access to all your files and emails. If you communicated by computer or phone with an activist organisation, a burglary or cyber attack might get access to their computers too.

One way to reduce the risk is to use a phone or computer on a once-only basis. You buy a device at a shop where no one knows you and you pay in cash, so there's no electronic record tying the purchase to you. You use the device for calls or emails or whatever — and then throw it out, far from home, with no fingerprints.

This is an occasion when it can be helpful to be extra cautious. The main thing is to think carefully about what the other side might do to track you down, and then take steps to remain invisible, or at least to create the possibility of plausible denial.

Surveillance techniques are ever more sophisticated, but so are methods of evasion, for example using encryption, stenography, proxy servers and anonymous remailers. Unless you're an information technology specialist, you can't be expected to learn everything that's possible. So use common sense to avoid obvious traps.

If you put your passwords on a slip of paper next to your computer, you're vulnerable. If you speak loudly on the phone about revealing secrets, in public when others can hear, you're at risk. Avoid the big risks first before worrying about advanced methods of cyber-surveillance.

Style

If you write your own account of events, be aware that your writing style might be used to reveal your identity. So you may wish to disguise your writing, which is not as easy as it sounds. Your writing might have some distinctive features, for example using certain words (or misspelling certain words), adding commas in a certain way, or capitalising certain words. Try to understand your own style, and figure out a way to disguise it. For example, you might run your text through a translator into another language and then back again. Or you might use voice recognition software instead of writing the text yourself, or vice versa. If you have a trusted friend, get them to edit your writing so it's no longer your characteristic style. If you are leaking your account to an activist group, ask them to edit the text to disguise your writing style.

Behaviour

Imagine that you've leaked documents, and the story has just hit the Internet, with lots of comment — including among your co-workers. They are all wondering who made the disclosure. Top management is about to set up an investigation. How should you behave at this time?

The answer is easy: behave just like you normally would. If you do anything differently — speak with a louder or softer voice, greet people differently, talk to different people than usual — others might suspect you are the leaker.

There's one thing you should do differently: you need to react to the leak as if you are not the leaker. So think how you might react if it had been someone else. (And, come to think about it, maybe one of your co-workers leaked the same documents.) Behave as surprised or perplexed or excited as you might otherwise be. If you're a low-key sort of person, then you shouldn't show much emotion; if you're talkative, then you should be talkative about this.

Under stress, it is challenging to behave "normally." When you don't pay attention to your own behaviour, it is easy enough. However, when you start paying attention to how you act, this can disrupt your usual patterns: you become self-conscious. The challenge is to relax even though you may experience great tension.

You have one big advantage: you can fake being normal better than you imagine. Inside, you may feel different, but most others will not notice anything. It's like when you get up to give a talk to a large crowd. You think everyone can tell you're nervous, but actually few will notice anything. So just carry on like usual and you can pull it off.

If there's an investigation and you are a prime suspect, then a different sort of acting is needed. You need to behave just like you would if you had been falsely accused. Imagine that someone else was the real leaker. If you're questioned, respond as if the leaker was this other person.

Maintain your nerve. Remind yourself that most leakers are never identified. Aim to be one of them.

Who to tell?

Many people, when they have a secret, have a great urge to tell someone else. When a co-worker passes on a juicy piece of gossip, do you immediately race to find someone else to tell? Think about the times when someone told you a highly personal and confidential story. Did you tell anyone else at all? If you don't keep secrets easily, you may find it difficult to leak successfully.

Sometimes, when leaking, it's best to tell no one. This is possible when you leak documents only. If you tell someone, you need to rely on them to keep the secret.

If you make personal contact and reveal your identity to a journalist or activist, you need to rely on them to maintain your anonymity. The more experienced the journalist or activist, and the better their track record in exposing problems, the more you can trust them.

Should you tell your family members? You need to decide how well they can keep a secret. It can be valuable to be able to discuss matters with those closest to you. However, if they start telling others what you've done, your identity might eventually be revealed to your bosses.

Should you tell your closest friends? Again, you need to weigh up the benefits and risks.

Should you tell your lawyer? This should be safe — but sometimes isn't. Your lawyer, or a friend of your lawyer, might work for the other side, namely your employer, and your employer has a lot more money than you do.

Choosing methods

Suppose you've decided that leaking is the way to go. How should you do it? Should you meet with a journalist, use email, set up a website ... there are several options. How should you choose? Here are some factors to consider.

Security. Who is going to find out? How easy will it be for you to deny it was you?

Convenience. It might be much easier to leak in some ways than others. Maybe phoning is easy, and secure too because you have a phone not linked to you. Maybe using a safe computer is awkward, because you need to go to another location, and doing so raises suspicions in your family.

Familiarity. If you're comfortable using a particular method, you're more likely to use it effectively. If encryption or secret meetings cause you to freeze up, try something you're used to.

Practice. If you're able to practise beforehand, you can improve at using the method and then, when you need it the most, you'll be much better at it. If you have a reason to contact activists, you'll know what's involved and have a better sense of who to trust. If your job allows you to practise methods for computer security, use the opportunity to improve your skills.

Sustainability. You've chosen a method to leak — can you keep using it, next week, next month or even years from now? If there's a need to keep leaking, you need a method you can maintain.

General availability. If you're part of a team of leakers, then your methods should be ones that two or more people can use. If one leaker is caught or leaves or needs to keep a low profile, then others can take their place. If you're a lone leaker, think about the example you set for your co-workers: some of them might feel inspired by your example. If the method you've used seems attractive to them — or even just possible — they are more likely to take it up.

The question "How should I go about leaking?" doesn't have a single best answer. There are all sorts of considerations to take into account, each one involving advantages and disadvantages. It's worthwhile to spend time and effort figuring out the way to proceed. You may decide not to leak at all, but if you do want to do it, choose a reasonable method and go ahead when the time is right.

Leaking can be very effective. Employers demonstrate this when they launch efforts to track down leakers. These efforts often end in failure: many leakers are successful, in that they get the information out and don't suffer reprisals. However, the efforts to track down leakers have a second goal: to scare workers so they won't leak. So think of this: how can you leak in a way that gets the message out and so the subsequent hunt for the leaker — for you — actually helps show the problem you're trying to expose? Maybe there's no way to do this, but if there is, it puts the employer in a bind: either just accept that leaking will occur, or search for the leaker and make things worse.

Conclusion

Leaking has two main advantages: you can get the message out without reprisals, and remain in the job to do more later, if needed. However, it's not an easy option. Often there are serious hunts to find the leaker, which means you need to take precautions and put up a false front. Leaking involves a degree of deception — you don't reveal what you've done — which needs to be weighed against potential gains.

The most important consideration for potential leakers is to plan ahead. This means thinking carefully about what information or documents to leak and who to send them to. It means anticipating the likely things the employer will do to track you down, and figuring out ways to foil them. It means being prepared to continue with your work as if you hadn't been involved. It means understanding your co-workers, your family, your friends and anyone else you think you might want to tell, and deciding whether telling them will help or hurt. Sometimes they are better off not knowing, and that can make it lonely for you the leaker. You need to decide whether this will feel acceptable for you emotionally.

If you plan far ahead, you can start learning about skills for leaking even though you think you'll never need them. You can learn about successful leaks, acquire computer skills, practise seeing whether people can keep a secret, and learn what sorts of material are best suited for documenting and exposing a problem.

If you help others to learn the same skills, then maybe one of them will become the leaker instead of you — and it will be harder to pin suspicion on any individual. The more people who know how to leak, the easier it will be for whoever decides to be a leaker. The more people who know how to leak, the harder it is for corrupt operators to hide what they are doing. Think of it this way: the more you and others spread the message and skills for leaking, the less likely any of you will ever need to do it.

Appendix: hotline services

Some companies provide a service to client businesses: they receive disclosures from employees and inform management about the problems. Suppose your employer subscribes to a hotline service called SC (Stop Corruption). You can email or phone SC with information about an abuse you've observed and SC will tell management — without identifying you. You may choose to identify yourself to SC, or remain anonymous.

These sorts of services are a combination of official channels and leaking. They are like official channels because your disclosure remains with management: there is no wider audience to provide accountability. They are like leaking because you can remain anonymous.

If the hotline service is managed by your employer, rather than an outside company, it is less likely to be effective, and your identity could be compromised. Beware!

To decide whether to use an independent hotline service, use all the precautions for both official channels and leaking. For example, try to find out the success rate of hotline disclosures. Are they acted on? How quickly? With what effect? Try to determine how well your identity is protected. If in doubt, take extra steps, such as ringing from a phone that can't be linked to you.

Hotlines are most likely to be helpful for problems that are not threatening to management, such as stealing by employees. When top managers are part of the problem, consider other options.

9 Building support

> Building support means getting others on your side. There are several important techniques, including:
>
> - preparing a written account
> - person-to-person approaches
> - support groups
> - action groups
> - letters
> - websites
> - using media.

The basic idea in building support is to win people to your point of view — namely that there is a problem and something needs to be done about it.

Of course, when you use official channels you are trying to win certain people to your point of view, namely those people in authority, such as managers, judges or politicians. The idea in building support, in contrast, is to take your message to lots of other people, such as co-workers, clients, neighbours and the general public.

To compare different approaches, it's useful to use diagrams. Let's start with the people and groups who have the most sway in society, including top politicians, heads of big corporations and influential figures in government departments, media, professions, unions and churches. I will call them powerholders.[1]

(diagram: oval labeled "powerholders")

Next, note that there are different groups of powerholders. Sometimes they support each other and sometimes they clash.

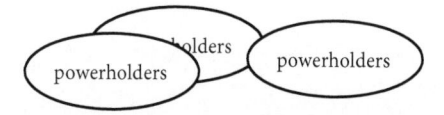

(diagram: three overlapping ovals labeled "powerholders")

Linked to one of the groups of powerholders is a policy or practice that is the problem you are concerned about. It might be due to:

- a decision the powerholders made and support, but you think has bad consequences for others

---

[1] There's no perfect term for these people. You might prefer a different label.

- "Elites." This may suggest, incorrectly, that these people are more talented than others, or better in some other way. Actually, the key distinction is that they exercise more power. So they might be called "power elites."
- "Decision makers." However, everyone makes decisions. Elites make decisions that have more impact.
- "Powerholders." Some critics say that people don't hold power; instead, they exercise power by getting others, by fear, habit or conviction, to do what they want.
- "The establishment." This suggests that powerholders are a solid, cohesive group, which may not be the case.

- a decision bad for everyone, powerholders included
- no decision where one is needed
- ignorance of the problem
- corrupt practice
- incompetent or bullying management
- other factors.

Whatever the case, you think this policy or practice needs attention, whether investigation, reform, abolition or replacement.

How can you bring about change? One approach can be called "appeal to elites." Basically, this means that you ask powerholders to take action.

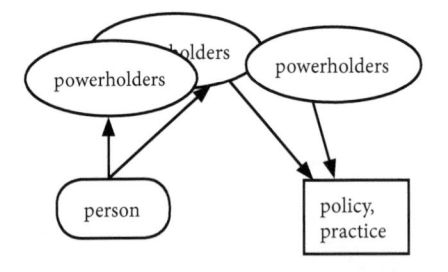

Direct appeal to powerholders

The classic example is writing a letter to the president or prime minister, or to heads of companies, government departments or television stations. The same approach is involved, in a lesser scale, in contacting the boss, the manager of a local shop or head of a sporting club.

This approach has a chance when you know the powerholder personally or when the problem is small or nonthreatening. If you are on good terms with the boss, a politician or the head of the local police station, you might be able to make a suggestion and have it taken up.

Lesley Pinson comments

In trying to gain the support of others and to get them to act, it is important to consider what might motivate them to act. What could they gain by acting? This might change the way you approach them. Others will have different interests than yours. For example, a politician might be more motivated to push for an investigation into your allegations if this would prove damaging to other political parties. You'll get further by providing a motivation for others to act than by simply demanding an investigation and expecting people to act accordingly.

When the stakes are higher and when you have no personal connections, your chance of success is tiny — even if what you suggest is eminently sensible. The trouble is that the powerholders are most strongly affected by each other and by the need to maintain their power.

Furthermore, from their point of view they have only a limited scope for action because of all the obstacles they face. A politician can receive more correspondence and reports in a day than they can read in a week with nothing else to do, and not have a hope of achieving more than a few of the many things they'd like to do. They might actually feel powerless themselves. They are high-level cogs in a *system of power*.

So your appeal is not heard. Another option is official channels. This includes grievance procedures, ombudsmen and courts, as described in chapter 7.

When you think about it, it turns out that all these channels were set up by the powerholders. They are meant to be independent, of

Using official channels

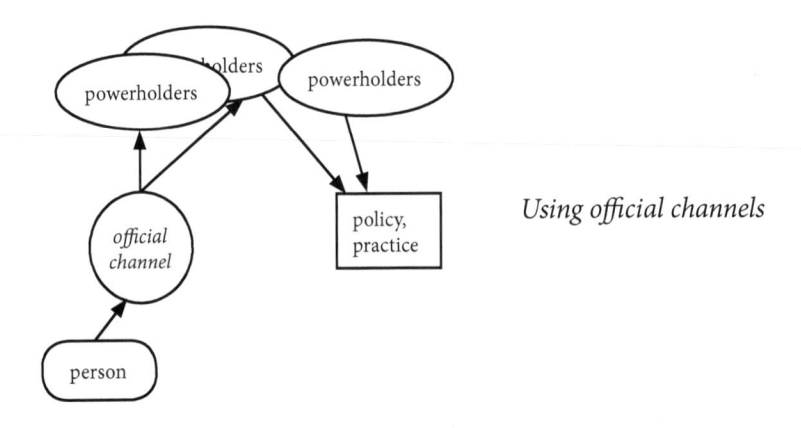

course, but in practice they have strong links with the powerholders. Your approach now is to be heard successfully through the official channels which, in turn, will influence the powerholders. Some official channels have quite a lot of independence, notably the courts. Others, like grievance procedures, may be independent in name but little else.

If evidence and logic aren't enough to get powerholders to act, an alternative is to apply pressure. You win the support of friends and co-workers. You get neighbours to sign a petition. You go on radio. You get an endorsement from local businesses and professionals. All of these individuals and groups demand change.

This is essentially what is called pressure group politics. Instead of using logic and evidence to persuade powerholders to act, other methods are used: letters, petitions, meetings, media coverage, voting, rallies. In pressure group politics, the aim is to use numbers and influence to get action from powerholders. Politicians often respond if they think popular support is at stake. Corporate executives often respond if they think sales are at risk. But there are no guar-

Pressure group politics

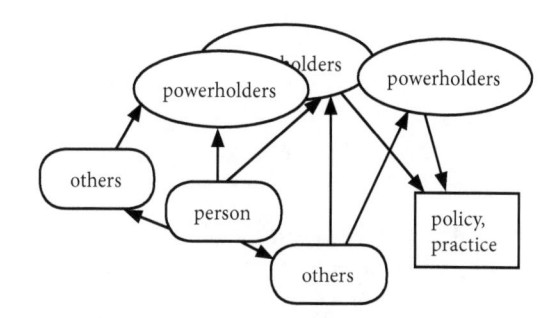

antees. Remember that powerholders are powerfully influenced by other powerholders. You might have massive popular support but some other group may have more money or inside influence.

Another option is direct action. Instead of getting someone else to act, you do it yourself, usually after gaining some popular support.

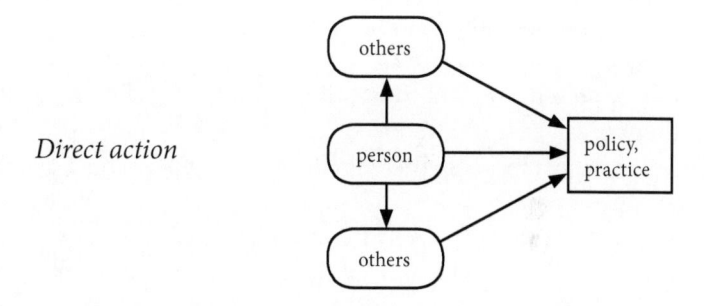

Direct action

Juanita was concerned about a nearby vacant block of land. It was overgrown and sometimes used as a dump. Recently there had been fights there between groups of youths. Since it was city-owned land, Juanita wrote to the mayor suggesting that the block be made into a park, greatly needed in this part of town. After six months she received a reply saying that her suggestion would be examined. She next tried the land commission, supposedly set up to deal with conflicting claims over land use. This also led nowhere. So she started talking to neighbours, organised a public meeting, wrote letters to the newspaper and even held a protest at the land commission offices. As a result of this agitation, Juanita found many supporters. She heard about similar problems elsewhere in the city. She also heard, from disgruntled city officials, that vacant blocks like this were purposely being allowed to run down so they could be sold off to developers at a low price, in exchange for pay-offs to politicians. Juanita continued to mobilise support. After lots of preparation, one day she and a large group of neighbours cleared rubbish from the site, cleaned it up, planted flowers and shrubs, installed recreational equipment, and started using the block as a park. However, early in the morning a week later, government workers cleared the site and put up a barricade to keep people out. The struggle was just beginning.

In this example, Juanita used four approaches: appeal to elites, official channels, pressure group politics and direct action. However, there's no requirement to use them in this sequence, or to use all of them. Each case is different.

In each approach, there is a need to win over some people.

- Appeal to elites. You need to convince the powerholders.
- Official channels. You need to convince relevant officials, such as judges.
- Pressure group politics. You need to convince various people, including individuals and leaders of organisations in the community, and win over some of them strongly enough so they will help. You don't have to convince powerholders, just put enough pressure on them to act.
- Direct action. You need to convince at least some people to be powerfully committed, enough to take direct action themselves.

If you have truth on your side but what you have to say is threatening to powerful interests, then appealing to elites or using official channels is very unlikely to work. You do have a chance of convincing other people though — those who are not compromised by the powerful interests. This is the process of building support. It's the main subject of this chapter.

Building support is obviously important for pressure group politics and direct action, but it is also important when appealing to elites and using official channels. If officials know there is a groundswell of public opinion on a subject, they are much more likely to respond to letters and formal complaints. Anyone planning to use official channels should be aware of the value of building support.

There are various aspects to building support, including approaching people, writing letters, and using the media. There's no fixed order for using these techniques, nor any necessity to use any of them. So the order I treat them here is just for convenience.

Preparing a written account

It's extremely useful to have a written account of your case or the problem that concerns you. It's not essential, since you can make do with telling people about the situation, giving them relevant official documents or news articles, and referring them to others. A written account, though, makes things a lot easier.

- Instead of having to tell each new person the entire story, you can give them the write-up.
- The write-up can be an organising tool, for example circulated along with a petition or sent to potential supporters.
- Journalists will present the facts more accurately if they can refer to a short treatment.

- The process of writing an account may help you gain a better overall grasp of the key features in the case.

What you need is a short treatment. One page is ideal. Two pages (fitting on one sheet of paper) are okay. If you have a longer treatment, it's helpful to have a short summary.

Jean Lennane comments

It is just plain rude to expect someone to read through a thick pile of documents — some files are five centimetres thick! — especially with no summary. Don't assume your case is so important that others must read it no matter how you present it. It is simply courtesy to make it easy for others to understand your case — and this can help win them over as well.

The first thing to decide is what the write-up is about. Many cases are incredibly complex, with many dimensions. You need to decide what you think is the most important issue and focus on that.

Gale became a friend and supporter to a young girl, Aleta, who had physical and mental disabilities. Some of the treatment that Aleta received from certain family members was terrible. Furthermore, government disability service organisations had an appalling record in addressing Aleta's needs. Gale, in standing up for Aleta, was criticised by various people and soon discovered that government bodies had a poor record in lots of cases. Gale decided to write an account to tell people about the problems. What should she focus on? Some possibilities are:

a) The story of Aleta's life: who she is and what she has experienced

b) Aleta's most imperative needs
c) What needs to happen to improve Aleta's situation
d) The failure of family and government to fully support Aleta
e) Gale's own problems in trying to support Aleta
f) General problems with government disability services

The answer depends on Gale's goals. If her primary goal is to help Aleta, the focus probably should be A, B or C with some points from D and maybe E. If her primary goal is to change government disability services, the focus should be F, possibly using Aleta's story as an illustration.

You also need to decide what to include. Usually there is so much material that it seems impossible to imagine a short treatment. How can years of struggle be summarised in a few paragraphs? There's no way every detail or example can be included. So you have to make some tough decisions. Here are some criteria.

- Every statement should be true. If anyone might dispute it (including by lying), you should have documentation to back it up.
- Items should be understandable to an ordinary reader — straightforward and not requiring special knowledge.
- Items should be clearly related to the main focus of the write-up.
- If possible, the material chosen should be able to be put together so that it tells a story. Alternatively, it should use evidence and logical argument to build towards a conclusion.

Gale decided to write an article about Aleta. She wrote down a long list of things that could be included, and then struck out the weaker ones.

- Gale had lots of information about Aleta's disabilities and health problems, including how they were diagnosed and treated, emer-

gency visits to hospitals and so forth. For example, Aleta had special problems with allergies due to her other disabilities. Gale decided to include only a basic statement about Aleta's disabilities. Most of the medical history wasn't relevant to the main story.
- Aleta had been assaulted on several occasions, almost certainly by one particular family member. But Gale had no hard proof of assault. So she included the fact that a doctor had documented severe bruising on Aleta that was very unlikely to be accidental or self-inflicted.
- Gale had a lot of information about how obtaining services for Aleta had been obstructed as a result of a ruling by a court that had been interpreted by an agency in a peculiar way, and only changed as a result of several appeals and an involved process involving several agencies. Gale decided that the complications of the legislation and administration of services would be too hard to explain in a short account, and so replaced them by a short statement summarising the net effect.

Having decided the focus of the write-up and what sort of items are to be included, it's time to write. If you are an experienced writer or have no worries about doing it, go ahead. On the other hand, if, like many people, you are not used to writing and are worried it will be horrible, here are a few suggestions.

- Imagine you are writing a letter about the case to a relative or friend — someone you feel safe saying anything to.
- Go ahead and write down everything. Don't worry about length or quality. Just keep writing. You can fix up problems later.
- If you have difficulty writing the first sentence, just start writing anything. "I'm having trouble getting started. That's because I don't know what to say first, and I'm worried about what it will look like. Should I start with …"

- Write for just 5 or 10 minutes and wait until tomorrow to continue. In a few days or weeks you'll have written plenty.

Getting a first draft is just the beginning of the process. Here's a typical sequence.

1. Write a first draft.
2. Revise.
3. Revise.
4. Revise.
5. Give the draft to a few friends and supporters, requesting their comments.
6. Revise in the light of comments.
7. Revise.
8. Give the revised draft to several other people for comments.
9. Revise.
10. Give the polished draft to specialists in the field to check facts.
11. Have someone check for defamation.
12. Revise.
13. Proofread (check spelling, grammar, etc.).
14. Print.
15. Proofread once more before distribution.

You may not need to go through such a lengthy process. Some experienced people can throw together an eloquent article in an hour or two. Journalists do it all the time. But if this is the first time you have written about this issue, then taking lots of care is wise and worthwhile.

It all may seem a lot of trouble just for a little article. However, it's not much compared to the money and effort you'd put in going through an official channel. A well-constructed article can be an incredibly potent tool.

Let's go back to the sequence. After step 1, the first draft, there are three types of steps: revision, getting comments, and proofreading. Revision means going through what you've written and improving it: checking facts and fixing the way you've expressed them; rewriting sentences to make them clearer; adding or deleting material; and checking spelling and grammar.

Be sure to include a title, if possible one that is short, descriptive and appealing. At the beginning of the write-up, it's often effective to have a summary, one or two sentences long. At the end there should be a concluding paragraph that contains the main points. You may also want to include some extras: references, further reading, photos or cartoons, and documents in support of your claims.

When you've done as much revising as you can, so you're not sure how to improve it further, it's time to obtain some feedback. Inviting other people to give you comments is vital for several reasons. You may be so close to the issue that you haven't explained basic things. This is quite common. Other people are fresher to the issue. Most of all, they are your potential audience, and they may be able to tell you how to communicate to them more effectively. If they are specialists in some area, they may be able to help with technical points.

Not everyone is good at giving comments. Ideally, you need someone who is sympathetic but skilled at giving you specific suggestions for improvement — such as which paragraphs to omit, what points to emphasise more, whether to reorganise the material, change the tone, etc. Your friends may be afraid to hurt your feelings and just say it's good. When this happens, ask them which parts they liked the most, and then ask which parts could be improved — and how. Then there are people who are critical but not helpful. If they say it's too negative or too complicated, ask which parts are causing the problem and how they might be changed.

Comments are just that: comments. You don't have to agree with them. You might think that some comments are based on ignorance or prejudice. Remember, though, that even ill-informed comments give you useful feedback. They show you are not communicating as well as you could to that person. Even if what you've written is accurate, you might decide to rewrite it so it communicates better.

As you get towards the final version, it's time to pay more attention to proofreading. This may seem a trivial matter, but even one misspelled word sends a signal to some readers that this text is not completely accurate. Check every detail yourself and get one or two others to do it too. With word processors, it's straightforward to produce professional-looking printing. So make it look nice. Get someone experienced to help if necessary. And because every time you do anything with a text, it's possible to introduce errors, it's worth proofreading the final version before making copies to distribute.

What about getting someone else to write your story? If they are keen, good at writing and sympathetic, it's an excellent option. You will have a little less control over the final product. On the other hand, someone not so close to the events may be able to prepare a more balanced and effective treatment.

Writing is one method of communication. It is also possible to produce audio or video records of your story. These could be for radio or television but also could be to post on YouTube. Producing effective recordings is a skill like any other, but unless you have experience in this already it's probably easier to produce a written account. Written text is far more efficient for conveying factual information: people can scan a page of writing to get a quick impression more easily than they can listen to a recording. On the other hand, recordings — especially video — can have a much more powerful emotional impact. If you become involved in producing audio or video, the same procedure as writing applies. The script needs to be written, revised, commented on and checked. It needs to be in a style appropriate for the medium — a good radio script is quite different from a text for reading. Then there are the stages of producing the recording, followed by editing, again a process requiring continued revision and polishing. If you follow this path, be sure to have full support from someone with plenty of skill and experience.

Person-to-person approaches

One of the foundation stones of building support is contacting people on a one-to-one basis. This is nearly always involved at some level or other. The key questions are who to contact and who should do the contacting.

It's easy to think that talking to someone about the issues is a straightforward matter that doesn't require any preparation. Planning your approach beforehand sounds like manipulation, right? Wrong! Manipulation means trying to get people to do something against their better judgement. You don't need that with truth on your side. You just need to be an effective advocate for your cause. Planning helps.

If you have come under attack, you are likely to be stressed and possibly traumatised. This means it's very hard to appear "normal" and to be an effective communicator. You may become nervous or depressed talking about the issue. The same applies if you are passionate about an issue and likely to become excited or angry. In this case, it may help to talk things over — your own emotional state as well as the issues — with a close friend, relative or trusted counsellor before you venture to approach others.

When it comes to talking to people about the issues, it can be useful to classify people into different groups. One useful breakdown is likely sympathisers, likely neutrals and likely opponents.

Likely sympathisers are people who probably agree with your views on the matter, at least in crucial areas. This may include friends, some co-workers and some outsiders. For example, if you are exposing illegal pay-offs in an organisation, likely sympathisers might include friends (except those with ties to the guilty parties), co-workers who are not implicated, and those losing money from the pay-offs.

Likely neutrals are people who wouldn't automatically take a stand one way or another, often because they don't know anything about it or don't know the people involved. In the case of the illegal pay-offs, this might include workers in a different division and most people outside the organisation.

Likely opponents are people who probably will oppose you. They may include those who, for whatever reason, dislike you, plus those who are threatened by your action on this issue. Those involved in the pay-off operation plus those who have covered it up, plus anyone you've alienated in the past, are likely opponents.

Before you approach anybody, it's worth deciding what you want to achieve and how you're going to go about it. It can be disastrous to arrange a meeting with someone and then dump on them at great length with a confusing story punctuated with anger, outrage and self-pity. Save the raves for those willing to support you emotionally.

With likely sympathisers, it can be appropriate to give a moderately lengthy account. But check first. If they are busy, be brief. But as well as telling the story, explain why you are telling it. Perhaps you are seeking their advice. Perhaps you'd like some support, such as signing a petition, writing a letter, commenting on a draft article, attending a meeting, speaking to others or to the media.

If you are seeking advice, say so at the beginning. If you are seeking support, it's often better to save requests until later, judging how responsive the person is as you go along. If they are very sympathetic, you can ask outright for support: "Would you be willing to write a letter?" If you're not sure, one technique is to describe what you're trying to achieve and how people can help. For example, "There's going to be a meeting next week to discuss taking action on the pay-off issue. If you know anyone who'd like to attend, here's the phone number of the organiser."

One of the most useful things you can get from sympathisers is advice. Those who have been through a similar situation or campaign before can be especially useful. Any time you're telling your story to someone, it is valuable to observe how they respond. Sympathisers, though, are more likely to give you hints on how to improve, especially if you ask. "Do you think we should focus on the Stringer pay-off or on the whole pay-off culture?" "Will a petition to the board be any use?"

In approaching neutrals, a suitable goal is to make them aware of the issues and more sympathetic to your point of view. Perhaps a few may be willing to take action on your behalf, but that shouldn't be the main goal. Rather, it is to change the general climate of opinion. The vast bulk of neutrals are people out in the community who know little or nothing about the issues. If you can convince them that illegal pay-offs are occurring, most will become more sympathetic to those doing something about it.

The general climate of opinion, in the long run, can be quite potent. It means that opponents have fewer sympathisers. It means that when the issue comes before a manager, a rival firm's owner, a judge or a politician, that person may have been influenced, either directly or by comments from a family member, a co-worker, a friend or client. When a person in a crucial position hears comments — "Did you know about the pay-off operation? It's a real scandal." — from a daughter or dentist, it may not make a difference. But sometimes it does.

Approaching opponents is also worthwhile. A reasonable goal is to make them less hostile, perhaps to become a neutral. It can be quite a challenge to approach those you think are responsible for problems and to present your viewpoint in a reasonable manner. Yet there is much to be gained if you can handle the situation. You don't need to be hostile or to expect a conversion. You can simply say you'd like to present your point of view and that even if they don't agree with it perhaps they can understand where you're coming from. This can be helpful since it is harder to demonise someone who is making a sincere effort to maintain dialogue. Of course, an extremely hostile opponent may interpret anything you say in the wrong manner and use any weakness in your case as a point of attack. If you think it's too risky, then don't make the approach, or get a sympathiser to do it.

If your case is long and complex — like most cases! — then a written summary is a valuable tool even with sympathisers. After reading the account, they can ask questions and you can amplify points that are especially relevant to them. For neutrals, a written account is even more valuable: it puts them in the picture quickly and efficiently. With opponents, a written account gives them your point of view in a precise way that might be hard to achieve verbally, especially if the meeting makes you very tense.

Creating a support group

A support group is a group of people who give emotional support to each other. Members of the group often have common experiences or goals. For example, there are support groups for women who have been sexually abused, for people with diabetes, and for whistleblowers. Alcoholics Anonymous is a type of support group.

The power of a support group comes from sharing common experiences. Many people who suffer from discrimination, disease or assault feel terribly alone — others just do not understand what they are experiencing. Meeting others in the same situation, and listening and talking about what they've gone through, is informative and helps with the healing process.

If a support group already exists that suits your situation, then attend and judge for yourself. If not, you can set one up. All you need is two or three other people in a similar situation. Set a time, invite people, meet and talk.

The best way to learn about how to make support groups work is to attend some and to talk to people experienced in running them. There are some standard patterns. People attending are allowed a fair opportunity to speak. Others listen without passing judgement. Confidentiality is expected (though there can never be absolute guarantees). Often there are rules (stated or assumed) about how long people speak, who can attend, what issues are addressed, etc. There is no need for office bearers, minutes, motions or voting. Meetings are for sharing experiences, not for conducting business.

Sometimes the biggest challenge is getting a group going. People may say they are coming but not show up. Size isn't all that vital. Even meeting with just one other person — or talking on the phone — can be very helpful.

Another problem is when a group gets large, perhaps over a dozen people. This means time for each person to speak is limited. A simple solution is to break into two smaller groups at the time.

To ensure a smooth operation, it is very helpful if someone involved has experience in facilitation of meetings. Sometimes there is a committed person who is willing to do this — who may or may not be someone with the same experiences as the others. Because people in support groups are often under a lot of stress, there can be conflicts. An experienced facilitator will be able to deal with difficulties. You can also consult books dealing with facilitation. Here are a few suggestions.

- Make sure everyone is introduced. A key part of any meeting is meeting people.
- Make sure ground rules are clear. Is smoking permitted? What time will the meeting finish? Who is facilitating? For sensitive and personal issues, it's often wise to request that people treat matters as confidential, but warn everyone that there can be no guarantees, so they should take that into account.
- Give everyone a chance to speak who wants to. This might be at each meeting or over a series of meetings. This may mean setting a time limit for each person's story. Even for the best facilitator, it can be a challenge getting a speaker who is passionate or distressed when telling their own story to operate within a strict time limit.
- If the aim is support, then hostile comments by others should be discouraged and openly countered. It can help to say that no one has to agree with anyone else, or believe someone else's story, and that the aim is to help each person to help themselves.
- Before finishing, make arrangements for any future meetings and be clear about who has responsibility for them.

A support group helps, in several ways, in the process of building support.[2] It puts people with similar concerns in touch with each other, gives them insights into the problem they confront, gives them the energy to keep going, and so can provide a launching point for action.

Creating an action group

As the name implies, the primary purpose of an action group is action — doing something to change things. "Action" can be defined in various ways. It can include:

- writing letters
- making phone calls
- face-to-face lobbying
- circulating petitions
- soliciting support door-to-door
- setting up websites
- holding meetings
- joining rallies
- speaking on street corners
- joining a strike, boycott or sit-in.

There are all sorts of action groups, such as environmental and human rights groups, of which the best known are Greenpeace and Amnesty International.

The primary aim of a support group is to help individuals by sharing experiences. An action group, in contrast, is oriented to doing things involving, or communicating to, people outside the group.

---

[2] The word "support" is used here in two related but slightly different ways. A support group provides mutual help, whereas "building support" means a process of winning allies.

In practice, the two are often mixed. Action groups provide support and some support groups decide to take action. There can be a tension between the two functions, and it's best to be clear just what is intended.

If you are interested in changing the system, first find out whether an action group already exists, even in a related area. For example, if you have discovered that a certain bank is misleading farmers and small businesses and stripping them of their assets, you should investigate any action groups that deal with the banking sector or, more generally, with economic issues or corruption. One of the best ways to find out what groups exist is to contact other groups. Activists often know what's happening outside their own area of special interest. Libraries have lists of community organisations.

If there's no group, you can start one. You just need to find other people who have similar concerns and call a meeting. If your concerns are specific, you may need to broaden the issue. Your personal interest may be in exploitative practices by a particular bank; you can broaden this to include all banks, all financial institutions, or even corporate exploitation of customers generally. There is value in campaigns that target particular organisations but there is also value in developing a broad picture of the problem.

What should an action group do? This is an enormous topic. There are lots of skills involved, such as writing media releases, motivating members, planning campaigns, maintaining a web presence, obtaining funds, running an office and organising vigils and rallies. The best way to learn such skills is through practice. Try to find an experienced activist who will give you tips, or join an action group — one you are in sympathy with, of course! — in order to learn skills. In most cities there are dozens or hundreds of action groups of all sizes, orientations and styles. In rural areas and small towns, there may not be so much to choose from. Nevertheless, there are usually some people who have experience in taking action. Ask around to find out who they are and then approach them to learn what you can. There are also some good books on taking action (see the references section at the end of this book).

An action group doesn't need to be large to be effective. In a group with a dozen members, often just one, two or three are the driving force and do much of the work. So if you have a group with just two or three activists, that is enough to accomplish a lot. Indeed, many groups that seem impressive on the outside are mostly the work of one dedicated individual who writes letters, produces a newsletter, organises meetings, and appears on the media.

Letters

Suppose you have exposed an operation in which trade licences are given to people without proper qualifications in exchange for various favours. There are attempts to discredit your claims, your work is put under intense scrutiny and you have been threatened with losing your job. If you write a letter to the top manager, that won't help much — that's where the threat came from! Also, a letter from you on your own behalf has limited impact because it can be dismissed as special pleading. But if someone else writes to the manager expressing concern about the licence issue and supporting your role, that's a different story. It accomplishes several things.

- It involves someone else supporting your stand.
- It shows the manager that someone else supports your stand.
- It provides an example to others of how they might support your stand.

The someone else can be called a "third party." The first and second parties are you and the manager (or perhaps the organisation as a whole). In a dispute between two parties, anyone else is a third party. Third parties are independent and often seen that way. The whole process of building support involves getting third parties to take your side.

When members of Amnesty International write to governments on behalf of political prisoners, their impact comes from being seen as third parties. They are "someone else" and they care. AI members don't write on behalf of prisoners in their own countries. One reason is that appeals have greater impact when they come from someone without any obvious personal stake in the issue. Another is possible danger from supporting local dissidents — also a relevant consideration in the case of whistleblowers.

In pursuing your own case, it is a great advantage to have someone else take initiatives on your behalf. The more independent the person seems to be, and the less they stand to gain, the better. A person's lawyers are not perceived as independent; after all, they are paid to be advocates. Family members or business colleagues are a little better. Someone from a field with a reputation for independence, such as a judge or scholar, is even better. Of course, reputations can be created and destroyed. Some lawyers can establish an aura of objectivity and some scholars can be discredited.

Back to the writing of letters. If one third party writing a letter to the manager has an impact, then the impact is increased if several others write letters. This shows the manager that quite a number of people know about the issue and are concerned enough to take the effort of writing.

How are you to get people to write such letters? You can, of course, talk to them, explain the case and give them information on

Karen Silkwood, a technician at a US nuclear fuel-rod factory, raised concerns about workplace hazards, and died in suspicious circumstances. She was played by Meryl Streep in the 1983 film Silkwood.

who to write to. At this point, having a write-up about the case, with a few documents to back it up, is quite effective. It also means that you can take the issue to wider audiences. For example, you can post your write-up to selected people in other parts of the country or the world.

Imagine you are a chief executive officer. Your deputy has reported that an employee, Jones, whose performance is suspect, has made scurrilous allegations about impropriety in a subsidiary. Which approach do you take more seriously?

The rave You scroll through a giant file sent by Jones. You read a few paragraphs, but it's not quite clear at first glance what the allegations are. You notice that Jones' document — an "open letter" — has been sent to dozens of politicians, government officials and prominent figures. It's filled with claims about corruption, denounced in CAPITAL LETTERS AND EXCLAMATION POINTS!!! In fact, you may not read this at all: your secretary might have eliminated it from your in-tray as not worthy of attention.

The concerned query Three letters have arrived in the past month from individuals expressing concern about the allegations that Jones has raised. They ask you to look into the matter personally with an open mind. They also say that they have the highest regard for Jones' integrity and performance.

The rave might be based on a foundation of facts, yet it is quite unlikely to be effective because it is not targeted, makes excessive and unsupported allegations, uses the wrong style and it comes from the aggrieved party. The concerned query is written personally addressed (to the CEO), is a query rather than a sweeping accusation, is modest in style and comes from someone who is apparently independent. The concerned query may not be effective either, but it has a better chance.

There is no single "best style." What's appropriate for a CEO is not what works best for a radio sound-bite. The point is that the style should be tailored for the audience and the purpose.

Sending letters, and getting others to send letters, can be a potent method of building support. Letters to a boss, administrator or politician may not change anything directly, but they do involve people taking action. To take the issue to wider audiences, letters can be sent to other organisations, action groups, people with a special interest in the area, and the media, among others. There are numerous variations. If someone is willing to give support by writing a letter, think carefully about where it might have the most impact. A letter to the president sounds good, but alternatives might be better. What about a letter to the newsletter of a trade union or professional association? A letter that is seen by many others is more likely to build further support.

Letters can be hand-delivered, posted, emailed or put online. The old-fashioned formal letter still has a certain edge in terms of presentation and impact — it can be posted or attached to an email. Email has the advantage of being very easy to send and reply to. By the same token, many people receive so much email that one more may be lost in the clutter. That's all the more reason to take a lot of care in presenting a clear and succinct message.

Websites

Nearly every business has a website — so why not a whistleblower? Putting material on the web makes it available to the world in exactly the way you want to present it. Potentially it's a huge step in building support. It's simple to do — at least it seems simple.

If you decide to put your story on the web, what should be included? The easiest way to start is with the write-up you prepared (discussed earlier in this chapter). It should be completely accurate, straightforward to read, and comprehensible to an outsider. Remember that web pages can be seen anywhere in the world, so your story might be read in Chile, Korea or Algeria. So make sure you say where and when things happened and briefly indicate the significance of local and national features such as organisations.

Most likely, your story is long and complex, so it is tempting to put the whole thing on your site. But first ask, "Who wants to read this?" Only a few people will be interested in the details of your case. More will be interested in the message from the story: they want to learn something about or from your experience. So you might want to have a take-home message, which could be about how the system works, what you did that made a difference or what you learned from the saga.

When people open a webpage, they immediately make a decision about whether to spend any time on it. The title is crucial, and so are the first few sentences. Have a look at other web pages to see what looks attractive and makes you want to read further.

You can provide a very long document if you want, but often it's better to present a short or medium-sized story, with links to supporting documents or a longer account. In this way, you provide a conveniently brief treatment for those want the basics, and a fuller treatment for those with a special interest in your case, or who need to be convinced of its credibility.

In general, quality is more important than quantity. Whistleblowers often want to tell their whole story, with every gory detail. This temptation should be avoided. Unless you are a talented writer, it will be hard to turn your story into a gripping epic. Furthermore, talented writers know that, in many cases, less is more: you tell what is needed to make a point, and no more. So when setting up a website, it is best to start with a short, accurate, clear account, and only add to it when you have additional good material.

Where should your web material be hosted? One option is to set up your own website. This is quite easy: a search will lead to many free website services. It's wise to choose a site hosted outside your country, in a place not susceptible to pressure. Otherwise your site might be taken down after your employer makes a complaint to the service provider.

Robina Cosser comments

Choose the name of your website carefully. It should be catchy and easy to remember, closely related to your content, but not too similar to the names of other websites.

Metatags are essential. They will make a big difference to the volume of traffic to your website.

Another option is to put your material on someone else's site. This can have the advantage of greater credibility or visibility, especially if your story is one of several similar ones. The site might already have a readership, so you don't need to work as hard to publicise your story. On the other hand, you may need to rely on someone else to update your documents. This may be okay if the site is run by a friend or relative acting on your behalf — someone who is sensitive and responsive.

Putting material on the web is like putting a poster on a wall — a wall with billions of posters! Hardly anyone will know your site exists unless you tell them. The easiest way to do this is by emailing them with the web address. Other possibilities include handing out business cards, putting the address in comments on blogs, and encouraging other site owners to make a link to your site.

Then there are search engines: they will automatically register your site, assuming someone else has made a link to it. You can make it easier by adding metatags to your webpages, giving a description and keywords.

One of the best ways to learn how to design an effective website is to look at a range of other sites, especially those by or about whistleblowers. You can get ideas for design, backgrounds, titles, summaries, links and web domains. Another good way is to seek comments from friends. Send them the link and ask which aspects of the site they like and which aspects could be improved. This will serve a dual function, letting them know about the site and obtaining feedback.

If your site is effective, you might come under attack. Opponents might make nasty comments in blogs. You might receive a threat to sue. Pressure might be put on your service provider to take down the site. One of the great advantages of a website is that you can easily modify the text, removing allegedly defamatory material, if that's what you choose to do. On the other hand, you can use the attack to generate greater attention to your concerns.

Using mass media

One of the most potent ways of building support is through coverage in the mass media — newspapers, radio, television, magazines. If you stick entirely to official channels, you may avoid the media (though it might get involved even then). If you use the strategy of building support, then you should consider using the media at some stage.

When trying to expose a problem, the media can generate awareness with dramatic speed. When faced with a corrupt or recalcitrant bureaucracy, media coverage is one of the few things that has a chance of denting business as usual. On the other hand, sometimes the media will refuse to touch a story. At other times they turn against dissidents and make things far worse.

If you're going to use the media, then it helps to understand their operations a bit. After all, organisations pay vast amounts of money, for advertising and public relations, to use the media for their own ends.

For the commercial media, there are two main driving forces to be aware of. The first is profit and is mainly the concern of owners and top managers. On the surface, the media's goal is to sell its message to readers and listeners; from a financial point of view, the media's goal is to sell audiences to advertisers.

The second important driving force is competition to get a good story, which is mainly the concern of journalists. Many stories are never run or are put on back pages, often due to shortage of space and audience attention and sometimes due to inhibition, such as the risk of a defamation suit. Journalists like to have their stories run, and run as prominently as possible.

The dynamics of media operation have led to the creation of a set of factors for what makes a good story. These are called "news values." Journalists and editors understand news values intuitively and will judge events by them instantly. Journalists and editors look for stories involving, among other things:

- local relevance
- human interest
- conflict
- action (especially for television)
- prominence (famous figures rather than unknowns)
- timeliness

- perceived consequences

If the president of the United States is impeached, it's a big story. If Buddhists in Sri Lanka have been promoting communal harmony for the past 20 years, there's no story. Complex stories pose a special difficulty and often are dropped or drastically simplified.

Stories about dissent and whistleblowing do have a chance. They involve personalities (human interest) and conflict, and sometimes prominent organisations. Current cases are far more newsworthy than old ones.

It's important to realise the news values involved. You might believe that the real issue is systematic discrimination due to deep-seated bias and distorted organisational structures. That won't get much attention, even though some journalists may be sympathetic. But if the issue is couched as claims of bias by several individuals who have been victimised as a result, then it becomes "a story." The personalities and conflict make all the difference.

Using the media thus involves compromises. You may think attention should be directed at the organisation and its deficiencies. The only story published might be about the treatment of an employee who spoke out.

Even with their limitations, the media can be a powerful force against social problems. That's primarily because they carry messages to large numbers of people, some of whom are likely to be sympathetic. The media thus are tools for building support. This is true even though many stories are distorted and unbalanced. In addition, many journalists and editors do care about the issues and do their utmost, within the constraints of media culture, to get a message across.

Official channels are designed to limit the number of people who know about a claim. They are a system that powerholders know how to handle, following procedures that are relatively predictable. In contrast, the media, by taking a story to all and sundry, are out of their control.

Those who routinely operate through official channels — such as lawyers — commonly advise against seeking media coverage. They are not trained and seldom skilled in using the media. More fundamentally, media coverage gets in the way of their methods. For lawyers, legal procedures are the way they know how to handle things, and other methods are a distraction or disruption. Some whistleblower laws specifically rule out protection if the whistleblower goes to the media before using official channels.

Don't let this deter you from using the media. If you're aiming to build support, you should always consider media coverage seriously.

Comparing methods

If you aim to build support, using the media is one approach — but not the only one. As we have seen, awareness can be fostered using face-to-face meetings, letters, petitions, leaflets, email, support groups and action groups, among others. It's worth comparing several of these.

	Control	*Audience*	*Credibility*
Letters	often great	targeted	often high
Websites	great	targeted + others	variable
Media coverage	low	general	fairly high

With letters and websites, what is said is controlled by those who write them. The audience of letters is mostly those who receive them directly, though people can make copies of letters. The audience of websites is those told about them, plus those who find them using links or search engines. The mass media, in contrast, cannot be controlled but often reach a much wider audience. Although many people are cynical about the media, a story often has considerable credibility. Note that these assessments are generalisations. For example, your letter may be badly written and have low credibility. On rare occasions, you may be so crucial to a major media story that you have some control over the way it's presented.

So, let's say you've decided media coverage would be a good idea. Before you approach a journalist or issue a media release, you need to be prepared. Here are some things to be prepared for.

- What are the facts about the case? Who, what, when, where, how?
- Who are you? You need to think about what you want to say about yourself.
- Are there any documents? Depending on the case, journalists may want copies.
- Is there anyone else to contact? This includes people who will confirm your claims and sometimes people on the other side. Have phone numbers ready.

If you have a concise write-up, it is a wonderful advantage — it can help a journalist make sense of the issue and get the facts right. But it's not essential.

Journalists are not an alien species. They are just people like you and me, doing a job as well as they know how. Most of them are friendly. Some will be highly sympathetic to your cause; a few may be hostile, perhaps due to their personal views or political affiliation. Most of them will behave professionally, within their own codes of professional practice. It helps to understand the pressures they operate under.

Time pressures. Most journalists are incredibly busy. They have to meet deadlines, after all. You may have a wonderful story to tell, but they don't have five hours or even half an hour to listen to it. Indeed, to be really effective you should be able to summarise the main points in the first minute of a conversation, or in the first couple of sentences in a media release.

Your case is the biggest thing for you, but a journalist may have a deadline in two hours with three stories to write. So be brief to start with and find out if there is a chance for a longer talk. If your case is a significant one, or if a journalist has the time to do a major investigation, there may not be quite as much of a squeeze on time. But that's the exception.

Journalists are usually in a rush. They may want interviews and documents immediately. Be prepared.

On the record. Remember that anything you say could potentially end up reported — even if you specify "background" or "off the record." If you don't want something reported, don't mention it. Journalists will try to steer the conversation in certain directions, seeking what they believe is the best story. You can follow if you're happy with the direction, but don't reminisce about your personal life unless you're willing to have everyone read about the most revealing anecdote.

Balance. Most journalists seek to present a "balanced" story. That usually means presenting both sides. After talking to you, the journalist may contact your worst enemy. Even a journalist who is very sympathetic to you may put in statements presenting the other side. So don't expect everything to go your way. If a story has nothing critical about you, it may appear unbalanced and lack credibility. Remember that a story that seems balanced to readers may seem incredibly unfair to the other side. If you are in a struggle with a powerful organisation, even the slightest criticism of the organisation is like a slap in the face of top officials.

Editing. Journalists do not have final control over their stories. An editor decides whether they get published and how prominently. Someone else writes the title. Sometimes the article is subedited, which may involve rewriting sentences and deleting paragraphs. If there is a potential for defamation, a lawyer may recommend changes or deletions. You won't get to see any of this. If the story doesn't appear at all, it may be because it was never written, because it didn't meet the editor's criteria ("news values"), because there wasn't enough space, or because it was deleted by mistake. If it appears, it may have been chopped and changed by various people. So don't blow up and curse the journalist or editor. Make an enquiry to find out what happened, and find out if there's anything you can do to help the process along.

It's worth visiting a newsroom to get a feeling for the overwhelming supply of information and of the rush, the chaos and the ease by which a story can be lost in the process. You want attention from the media, but so do lots of other people.

Angles. Journalists and editors need a peg on which to hang your story. It's not timely to report that corruption has been going on in the department for years. But if you've just sent a letter to the department head documenting some instances, the letter can serve as a peg. Journalists have a good idea of what "angles" can be used to make something into a story. You can help, sometimes, by suggesting ideas or by taking actions that provide angles, such as writing a letter, releasing a report or holding a meeting or rally.

Media coverage comes in fits and starts. You can be besieged by demands from the media one week and then ignored the next. Part of the reason is that media channels feed off each other. For example, staff at many radio stations go through the newspapers every day searching for people or stories they might want to follow up. So if there's an article about your case in a major daily, then you might well receive calls from several radio stations soon after, inviting you to be interviewed. (Less often do newspapers take their cue from radio or TV programmes.) Another part of the reason is that when a story "breaks" — first becomes reported — it is seen as worthy of coverage. A few days or weeks later, depending on the issue, it is dated and no longer considered newsworthy.

This is when it can become clear that the media are using you and your story just as much as you are using them. You know that the issue that concerns you is ongoing and deserves continuing attention. But from the media's point of view, it is probably only of short-term interest. It might be a one-day wonder.

A person with plenty of skill in generating coverage can, to some extent, overcome the media's short attention span. First, it's necessary to provide an ongoing flow of newsworthy material. For example, if you have documentation about abuses in an institution, sometimes it can be effective to release it bit by bit, over a matter of months, rather than in one batch. If you are using official channels, this can be dramatised: a submission, some testimony, a visitor commenting on the case, a protest meeting — each step can be promoted as a story. Another important part of keeping a story in the media over time is working with individual journalists. After they have studied the issue enough to write a story, then a follow-up is relatively easy. They may also develop a commitment to the issue. What you have to do is continue to supply them material and access, and not offend them by giving a big scoop to someone else.

Do you have to stick with the same journalists? What if they don't seem to be treating you fairly? There are implicit rules and expectations that apply. If you're new to the game, you can't be expected to know them. So ask. Ask people with experience in using the media, and ask journalists themselves.

If you start receiving media coverage, it can seem like a great thing. It can even become addictive! It's healthy to remember that media coverage is not the goal. It's only a means to an end. In this case it's a component of a strategy to build support. Building support is a method for helping deal with the problem you're concerned about.

Sometimes the media make thousands of people aware of an issue, making it difficult for powerholders to continue as before. On other occasions the media may seem to have no impact at all — a flash in the pan. Media coverage is not a cure-all.

Sometimes a story in the media builds support in an obvious and practical way, by leading to contacts. Someone reads a story in the newspaper or hears you on the radio and contacts you. Maybe the same thing happened to them. Maybe they have more information. Maybe they need help or advice. Maybe they want to help.

The media are tools to put you in touch with others with similar interests. You might spend years discussing your case with friends and acquaintances, yet only reach a few hundred people. One media story might be all it takes to put you in touch with a like-minded person outside your normal circle of contacts. Members of support groups and action groups know that media coverage is one way to bring in new members.

Media coverage is frequently a powerful tool for whistleblowers — but not always. On some issues, it is impossible to obtain media coverage. There are several explanations.

- Your story might not be newsworthy. It could be too old, too narrow, too amorphous or too complex. You need to see whether there's an angle that could be taken up.
- Your story might create too great a risk of defamation. If publishing a story opens a media company to costly litigation, this is a deterrent. The story can go ahead if the likely benefits — wider circulation, greater prestige — outweigh the likely costs. But if the facts aren't quite solid enough, if the target is known for suing, or if it's only a minor story to start with, legal risks can sink it.
- Your story may threaten powerful interests that have direct or indirect influence with media interests. Say you're exposing a company for false advertising. If the manager of the company is friends with the editor of the newspaper, that may eliminate the prospect of a story. Or perhaps the company runs a lot of advertising in the paper. In many small towns and some cities, there are close links between top people in business, government, media, professions and other fields. Your opponents may have powerful friends and this may rule out local media coverage. If you are trying to expose bias or corruption in the media themselves, getting media coverage is even harder.

If your story is newsworthy but is suppressed due to the local establishment, one solution is to look to media without local ties. If the city's newspaper won't touch your story, what about a newspaper in another part of the country, or a national newspaper? It's also possible to go international, especially if there are specialist outlets for your issue. Sometimes an article in a newspaper or magazine published in another country is the best way to open up the issue locally.

Remember again that media coverage is not the goal in itself. The strategy is to build support. If the media won't touch the issue, then you need to rely on other methods such as letters, social media and action groups.

An even worse scenario is that the media launch a concerted, unscrupulous, unbalanced attack on you and your cause. This sometimes happens, whether you are trying to use the media yourself or not.

Lesley Pinson comments

It's very important to decide whether you want to use print or electronic media — newspapers and magazines or TV and radio. Each has a different way of presenting a story and requires different things from you.

You may or may not be willing or confident enough to appear on TV or to conduct a radio interview. TV also depends on visual effects. A story about illegal dumping or faulty equipment would provide useful footage for TV whereas a story about financial fraud might provide little for TV to present visually.

TV and radio often follow print media and thus a newspaper story may lead to greater overall coverage by TV and radio. Also, an article in a local paper can lead to the mainstream media picking up on the story later.

You will have differing levels of control over what is published, depending on which media you choose to use.

It is worth monitoring different papers, radio programmes and TV shows to see how stories are presented and which types of stories are being told. If your story has political implications, some papers are more left or right wing than others.

It is also worth being aware of who is sponsoring (via advertising) various media outlets. Some commercial TV stations and newspapers, for instance, may be reluctant to publish a story that is critical of one of their major advertising clients.

Whilst monitoring different media outlets, it is worth making a note of various journalists who have presented similar stories or who have presented stories in a way that appeals to you. Direct contact with a journalist who you feel might be sympathetic to your story, or have some knowledge of the issue from previous stories, is far more likely to achieve a result than a completely cold call. It also won't hurt to appeal to the journalist's ego with some reference to their previous work, especially something just published. This is a useful way to start the conversation.

The ongoing struggle

The strategy of building support is seldom a short-term solution. Indeed, it is best seen as a process rather than a solution. In the long term, social problems will only be solved if lots of people become aware of them and are willing to take action. If your concern is bias in a single appointment, then by the time you build support it may be too late to do anything. But if your concern is bias in appointments as an ongoing problem, then building support has real potential. For the ongoing struggle, there are several things to keep in mind.

The struggle has phases and ups and downs. There can be periods of intense action and periods when nothing seems to happen. Interest in taking action can rise and fall. By being aware of this, you can avoid being too optimistic during the up phases or too discouraged during the down phases.

Defence and initiative are both required. If you are having any impact at all, you are likely to come under attack. You may be harassed, lose your job, be the subject of vicious rumours, or even come under a concentrated media barrage. Defending against such attacks is vital. At the worst times, return to basics. Review your goals. Consult with your most loyal supporters. Make plans based on building support. If the attack is unfair, and you can show that it is unfair, you can use that to build support.

As well as defending against attacks, you need to take initiatives, otherwise the agenda is always set by your opponents. Again, review your goals, consult and make plans.

Be ready to reassess your strategy. If your strategy doesn't seem to be working, make a careful examination. Is it because you aren't doing it right, because the other side is too strong, or because it's a bad strategy? Even if your strategy seems to be working, it may be worth examining. Perhaps you can do better. Perhaps there's a trap looming.

Appendix: the sabotage option

- A systems analyst leaves a firm but leaves behind a "logic bomb" that, half a year later, introduces systematic errors into the firm's computer files.
- A blast furnace operator, by purposely not making quite the right adjustments, allows a shutdown to occur, at great expense.
- A lawyer, about to leave his company, sends out bogus letters to clients under his head's name, undermining the reputation of the firm.

- A warehouse employee switches off the electricity for the cold room over the weekend.
- A packaging worker adds a slip of paper with an unpleasant message to thousands of gifts posted out to competition winners.

These are examples of sabotage at work. Such sabotage has a long history, and can be found in all manner of occupations. Sometimes workers, under intense pressure, can only obtain relief by disrupting or destroying machinery, and the person who does it has wide support. Sometimes a single disgruntled employee takes action as a method of revenge.

Is sabotage a useful option for dealing with problems such as corruption? Usually not.

There are some cases where sabotage can never be justified. For a mechanic to "fix" a car so it breaks down could put someone's life in danger. For a farmer to poison a neighbour's property is environmental vandalism. For a doctor to purposefully make an operation fail amounts to assault or murder. These sorts of criminal tactics are sometimes used against whistleblowers and social activists.

Few whistleblowers even think of sabotage as an option. They are often the most committed and hard-working of employees, with pride in doing their jobs well. To do less than one's best for others is repellent.

Nevertheless, after being treated in the most abominable way by a management that cares only about its power and is willing to do anything to cover up problems, even the most conscientious employee may begin to have dark thoughts of revenge. There are several reasons, though, why sabotage is not a good strategy.

- Sabotage seldom tackles the problem in a direct way. If a company is corrupt, then wiping its computer files certainly causes havoc

but does little or nothing to expose the corruption or institute a process to overcome it.
- Sabotage usually has to be carried out in secrecy. This means that it has to be an individual or small group operation, with little chance of involving large numbers of people. Hence it is a poor way to build support, since sympathisers can only observe rather than participate.
- Sabotage can lead to increased support for management and antagonism towards the saboteur. If co-workers or clients are seriously inconvenienced, they may turn against the person they believe is responsible. So powerful is this effect that sometimes a scheming management will carry out the sabotage itself but blame it on someone else. The same thing happens when an agent, for example paid by the police, joins an action group or attends a rally and tries to provoke violence, knowing that violence by protesters often discredits them.

Thus, there are some strong reasons against sabotage as a strategy to fix problems. However, sabotage can't be ruled out automatically. For example, many factory workers in occupied Europe under the Nazis worked slowly, made more mistakes than necessary and sometimes wrecked equipment, at great risk to themselves, all in an attempt to reduce output that served the Nazi war machine.

An ethical resister can ask several questions in making a decision.

- Could sabotage lead to risks to physical or mental health or the environment? If so, it's not appropriate.
- Does sabotage help solve the problem? If not, it's not a good method. (Is the main reason revenge?)
- Does sabotage have significant support? If not, it's likely to make people more antagonistic.

- Are there any alternatives to sabotage, especially alternatives that build support? If so, they are probably preferable.

Ironically, honest attempts to point out problems are often called "sabotage" or "treachery." If corruption is deep-seated, then exposing it does indeed undermine the usual way of doing things. It's important to go beyond the rhetoric and name-calling and look at who and what is serving the public interest. In most cases an open and committed stand against corruption and bad practice is far more threatening to vested interests than covert wrecking. To turn around the language, it is vested interests who are the real "saboteurs."

10 Case studies: considering options

> These case studies illustrate problems and strategies in:
>
> - workplace injury
> - scientific fraud
> - bullying
> - financial corruption
> - police corruption
> - sexual harassment
> - an unresponsive anti-corruption agency.

The following case studies illustrate the process of working out a strategy. Any single case study cannot easily illustrate multiple strategies. To partially compensate, I've introduced various "exits," where the story would take a different direction following a particular choice. The early exits are actually the most common outcomes — almost always unsuccessful.

Insiders and outsiders

These case studies focus on insiders: people closest to the problem, often working for an organisation. They face the greatest challenges and have the greatest risk of failure. However, in each case study there is a role for outsiders who want to take action. Outsiders usually are relatively safe from reprisals (though there are exceptions such as tackling organised crime). Outsiders therefore have more opportunities for acting openly. On the other hand, outsiders often lack the detailed information available only to insiders. Combining the insights of insiders with the actions available to outsiders can produce a powerful force for change.

A case of workplace injury

John worked for a major electrical company in a section that constructed and tested large transformers. After several years, he obtained a promotion and was put in charge of testing a big and urgent order. His duties required him to assume awkward positions, including exerting force with his hands above his head. John began developing pains in his right forearm. However, being extremely conscientious, he persisted working for long hours through the pain, which soon became much worse. Eventually he was unable to work without extreme pain, which radiated up through his elbow and shoulder and began appearing in his left forearm.

> ⇒ *Exit 1*. John arranges for another worker to finish testing the urgent order. He then resigns and spends several years off work before his condition begins to ease.

⇒ *Exit 2.* After reporting his problems to his supervisor, John is dismissed for failing to finish the urgent order. He spends several years off work before his condition begins to ease.

⇒ *Exit 3.* After reporting his problems to his supervisor, John is put on "special duties" that supposedly take his injuries into account. However, he is victimised in various small ways, sometimes being given tasks that are far too difficult to complete (even if he had been fully fit) and sometimes being given boring and pointless jobs. When he requests equipment to do his job, it doesn't arrive or he is given incorrect items. He encounters problems obtaining leave (which had never been a problem before), is asked to fill out forms over and over (copies are supposedly "lost"), is repeatedly transferred to different locations, put on inconvenient shifts and given no sympathy by his supervisor. In the face of this petty harassment, eventually he decides to quit.

John decides to put in a workers' compensation claim. He scrutinises the workplace's occupational health and safety agreement and finds that management has been negligent: it should have, but didn't, provide special equipment to reduce the risk of strain, institute mandatory work breaks and warn workers of the initial symptoms of overuse injury. He discusses the situation with several co-workers.

⇒ *Exit 4.* Management finds out the John is preparing a workers' compensation claim. Rumours are spread about him being a poor performer and malingerer who has manufactured claims about pain to divert attention away from his own failure and who is out to benefit his pocketbook at the expense of others. John is so distraught by the rumours that he leaves without pursuing the compensation claim.

⇒ *Exit 5*. At the workers' compensation hearing, lawyers for the electrical company produce evidence of John having been in a minor car accident ten years earlier, which they claim was responsible for his problems. John is successful nevertheless. The company appeals the decision, and the appeal board reduces his benefits considerably.

John has another option: pursuing a civil court action on the grounds of negligence. He finds out about what sort of evidence is required, and talks to some co-workers about testifying on his behalf. He obtains photos of the workplace and typical transformers. He asks about lawyers and is directed to one experienced with similar cases. He prepares a comprehensive case.

⇒ *Exit 6*. In court, John's case begins to fall apart. Only one of his supportive witnesses is willing to testify; the others are too afraid. Several managers and co-workers testify against him, claiming that he never worked long hours and never complained about pain or disability before taking sick leave. The electrical company presents documents showing that special equipment had been purchased and installed well before John began work on the urgent order. (It is obvious that the dates on these documents had been falsified.) His own photos are claimed to be from an earlier period. His case fails.

Before he goes to court, John makes contact with a workers' compensation support group and meets many others with stories like his own. He learns that corporate negligence is commonplace, as are injuries and dirty tricks to discredit those who make compensation claims. He obtains a lot of helpful advice on countering court claims. He compiles a dossier on his own employer. With help from one reliable current worker and several former workers with cases like his own, he obtains documents that will counter any falsified ones the electrical company might use. He goes to court and wins a substantial amount in damages.

⇒ *Exit 7*. The electrical company appeals. Meanwhile, employers have been pressing the government over mounting costs due to overuse injury cases. The government itself is a major employer, many of whose workers are making claims. The government puts a low cap on damages payable through civil courts, making it impossible to obtain suitable compensation.

⇒ *Exit 8*. The electrical company offers a settlement. John will receive a substantial pay-out, but he must agree to a clause preventing him from saying anything about the case or the size of his pay-out. Due to his inability to work, he accepts the settlement. Later, though, he is distressed to learn that another worker at the company develops an injury because proper equipment and systems have still not been installed.

Analysis. Employers often attempt to discredit workers who suffer injuries. A small minority of workers' claims may be contrived ("malingering") but the bulk are genuine, and often the employer is culpable. Employers can always deny responsibility for an injury; in addition, sometimes they dispute the very existence of an injury, as in the case of bad backs, overuse injuries and stress. For a lone worker to take on an employer or insurance company that is attempting to avoid paying compensation can be as traumatic as the original injury.

What outsiders can do

Join or set up a workers' compensation action group.

A case of scientific fraud

Sarah, a talented researcher with several years of postdoctoral experience, obtained a contract position in a major lab, where she worked with several others including the prolific Dr Williams. Sarah was a hard worker but she could not believe the tremendous rate at which Williams produced results. One day, while glancing at his lab books, she noticed a curious pattern. It appeared that half of his results were duplicates of the other half. This made it seem that he had done twice as many tests as he actually had.

⇒ *Exit 1.* Sarah says nothing. When pressed for time she occasionally starts duplicating her own results just like Williams.

⇒ *Exit 2.* Sarah comments to Williams about the results. He passes it off as a fluke. The next day Williams' current lab book no longer displays the duplicates and all previous books are locked away. Sarah gets a bad report and is terminated at the first available opportunity.

Sarah, having read about some cases of scientific fraud, knows that she must obtain proof. Over the next four months, she is able to photocopy hundreds of pages from Williams' lab books. There are quite a number of instances where half or two-thirds of Williams' data are copies of an initial data set (presumably valid). She makes several sets of copies and gives one set to a trusted friend.

⇒ *Exit 3.* Sarah gives all the evidence to the senior scientist in the lab. He dismisses the duplications as insignificant. He says the basic results are correct and have been confirmed by other labs. The only effect is to change the size of some of the error bars. She writes to the journals that published Williams' research. They do not respond. She writes to their scientific society and gets a noncommital response. Sarah gets a bad report and is terminated at the first available opportunity.

"...SO YOU WANT TO BLOW THE WHISTLE, HEY?... WELL, LET'S GET A FEW THINGS STRAIGHT...HAVE YOU GOT A LAW DEGREE, ALL THE EVIDENCE, THE SMOKING GUN, DID YOU SEE THEM DO IT, HEAR THEM PLAN IT... IF NOT, YOU CAN SHOVE OFF!..."

⇒ *Exit 4*. Sarah tries to build support by talking to other researchers in the same lab. It's not long before Williams finds out. Sarah is transferred to menial duties, her equipment is tampered with while she is away, and rumours are spread about her dishonesty and psychological hang-ups. She cannot stand the strain and resigns.

Sarah investigates the issue of scientific fraud. She soon learns that formal procedures for addressing scientific fraud hardly ever work and that the accuser often pays the penalty. She decides to lie low for the time being and gather evidence and support. She consults a statistician who agrees to analyse the data and finds that in nearly every case, an initial set of data is reproduced two or three times. But usually the duplicated points are not in the same sequence and so not readily identifiable by casual observation. She also consults with some senior scientists who are known for their investigations into scientific fraud. They say that Williams' actions are definitely improper. Fiddling with data is not uncommon, though the total scale of Williams' faking is unusual.

Sarah writes up a concise, rigorous treatment of Williams' fraud, backing it with sample data sheets. She prepares a plan of action to ensure the issue is not covered up.

⇒ *Exit 5*. She waits until she is reappointed to a five-year post, with a promotion, and then takes her report to the head of the institution for a meeting. The head promises to seek independent opinion and to keep the matter confidential. Within a week it is obvious that Williams has a copy of her report, so she goes as planned to the media, where a science reporter has been primed with the story. A blitz of newspaper and radio coverage causes a storm in the institution, which sets up a formal investigation — into both Williams and Sarah! She finds that some of her lab books are missing. She is accused, among other things, of inadequate documentation of her own research, of false claims for expenses, and of a false statement about a publication in her curriculum vitae when she first applied for a job. The internal inquiry is a whitewash of Williams. Sarah, under constant scrutiny at work, ponders whether to continue, to make an appeal for an independent inquiry, or to leave.

Sarah waits until she obtains a job at another institution. After settling in and finding that cheating is not carried out or condoned, she consults with her boss about exposing Williams. Her boss says the publicity will detract from their research, but she also says she'll support Sarah if that is what she decides to do. After discussing the matter with all of her new colleagues, she releases her report to the media. So — the same publicity, the same accusations about Sarah, the same whitewash. Sarah's career is held up somewhat, but she has achieved one important aim without massive cost to herself.

Analysis. Exposing scholarly fraud — whether it is fudging data, plagiarism or falsification of credentials — can be extremely risky. In developing an effective strategy, Sarah had to decide whether to use formal channels. She also had to decide who to talk to. Williams was charming, talented and ambitious, and had so many supporters that it was risky talking to anyone in the institution. As a result, she was best able to build support from independent scientists and through media coverage. If the media had declined to report the story, she could have circulated her report to scientists in the field, perhaps with considerable effect.

What outsiders can do

Bring together scientists who have been victimised for speaking out about fraud. Find scientists willing to comment on fraud cases and journalists willing to investigate them.

A case of bullying

Steve worked in a government department in a large section dealing with trade policy. He was experienced and got on well with his co-workers. Things changed when a new boss, Joe, was brought in from another department. Joe was talented, with a reputation for being a task-master. He could be charming but also had a dark side. He would suddenly turn on individuals, shouting and swearing at them. At staff meetings he would sometimes humiliate an individual by making cutting comments about their work.

Steve soon noticed a pattern. Joe never attacked those who were totally compliant and who were no threat to him. But anyone who showed a bit of independence and talent was a likely target.

⇒ *Exit 1*. Steve decides to stay on Joe's good side, does his bidding and informs Joe about people who are "stepping out of line."

> ⇒ *Exit 2*. Steve leaves for another job as soon as possible.

Steve does not want to leave, for two main reasons. He enjoys the work, and he is concerned about some of his co-workers who are also friends.

Over a period of months, Steve learns more about Joe's method of operation. Joe's fierce verbal abuse has lowered morale; several vulnerable workers have resigned or gone on leave for stress. A few who have attempted to stand up to Joe have suffered from sustained harassment. Joe finds minor flaws in these individuals' work and demands that it be redone. He arranges assignments so workers are likely to fail, and then explodes at them when they do fail. Few can survive such a sustained attack on their competence.

> ⇒ *Exit 3*. Steve tries to match Joe at his game, and exchanges shouts and insults with him in a major confrontation. Within the next month, Steve is set up for an embarrassing failure, receives a formal reprimand and is given a choice: transfer to a lesser post or resign.

> ⇒ *Exit 4*. Steve has a "heart-to-heart" talk with Joe, informing him of the destructive effects of his behaviour. Joe seems to listen, but later Steve is set up for an embarrassing failure, etc.

> ⇒ *Exit 5*. Steve goes to talk to Joe's boss, asking for some intervention. Joe's boss says Joe is producing results and that

> Steve should just get on with his job. Steve is lucky. If Joe's boss had told Joe about the meeting, his job would have been on the line.

Steve does some investigating. He talks to people who worked under Joe in his previous jobs. His style was the same then. He was able to intimidate his subordinates but charm his superiors, and his talent and hard work won him promotions in spite of the trauma and demoralisation he left in his wake.

Steve begins keeping a dossier on Joe. He talks to Joe's victims and writes up accounts. Because he is experienced and trustworthy, most of them are willing to sign the accounts when Steve promises not to use them without permission. Steve finds that some of Joe's actions verge on assault, such as when he grabbed one person's shirt and threw something towards another.

Steve also finds that Joe makes mistakes himself. Some of his decisions are flawed, and he sometimes misuses funds for his own advantage. This is minor-level abuse of privilege, but it reveals a major double standard considering Joe's finding of fault with others.

> ⇒ *Exit 6.* Steve submits a formal complaint about Joe, using testimony from several co-workers, to the department's internal grievance committee. During the investigation, Joe shows only his good side. The grievance committee is uncritical of Joe, and recommends only some shuffling of duties and meetings with outside mediators. Top management doesn't bother to implement even these recommendations. Joe begins a focused and subtle harassment of every individual whose testimony was in the complaint. (He has found out several names from material

given "in confidence" to the grievance committee.) Steve is the prime target, but survives because Joe is promoted to another department.

Steve begins to collect information about bullying at work. He learns that some bosses, when they perceive threats to their professional competence and survival, for example when subordinates do not measure up to expectations, respond with interpersonal aggression. He finds that in his department such individuals are usually tolerated and that management always sides with bosses against subordinates, no matter how outrageous the boss's behaviour.

⇒ *Exit 7*. Steve prepares a summary of key points about bullying, its effects and how to respond to it. He circulates copies to all his co-workers, and this encourages some of them to resist. He finds two others who are willing to work with him to formulate a strategy to deal with Joe. Joe tries every trick he knows to break up the group, befriending one and harassing another. The struggle continues.

⇒ *Exit 8*. Steve prepares a statement about Joe's behaviour, making sure that every statement is backed up by documentation. After taking a job in the private sector, he circulates copies of the statement throughout his old department and Joe's new department (Joe has been promoted). The statement severely cramps Joe's style. Joe sues Steve for defamation.

⇒ *Exit 9*. Steve, at a social function, meets a top manager and cautiously raises concerns about what to do about damaging behaviours. The manager has just heard a presentation about how to change abrasive bosses, checks out Steve's information and calls in a consultant to work with Joe. It turns out Joe didn't realise how much he was hurting others and gradually learns skills in more effective people management.

Analysis. Bullying bosses are very damaging, yet managements seldom are willing to act against them. Building support is difficult when bosses use divide-and-rule techniques. Yet if no one stands up to bullying, the problem will just continue.

What outsiders can do

Circulate information about bullying. Set up a bullying support group.

A case of financial corruption

Chris had years of experience as an auditor in financial institutions. After joining a major bank, she gradually became aware of an operation involving a Third World country, "Dalenz." Special low-interest loans were being given to the Dalenz government against bank policy, since these were high-risk loans. Payments from Dalenz — not loan repayments — were being made to the bank and put into a special fund, which top bank officials used for personal assistants, cars, family holidays, cruises and lavish parties.

When Chris asked a co-worker about the situation, she was told that this was standard practice for Dalenz — all the other banks did the same — and that the perks provided by the special fund were a part of the remuneration package for bank executives. It was simply a matter of convenience that it drew on Dalenz money.

⇒ *Exit 1*. Chris does her best to make the Dalenz operation appear normal financially and to get to a position where she can use the special fund.

⇒ *Exit 2*. Chris arranges for a transfer to another section. She's suspicious about the Dalenz operation but doesn't want to risk her job.

Over a matter of months, Chris finds out more about the Dalenz operation. By reading reports of Amnesty International and searching the web, she finds that Dalenz is a brutal dictatorship known for torturing dissidents and exploiting the workers. She also finds that the standard executive remuneration package includes only some of the perks paid from the special fund. She is sure it is improper for Dalenz money to go into the special fund.

⇒ *Exit 3*. Chris talks to the head auditor at the bank about her concerns, and expresses her belief that the loans should be stopped and Dalenz money not accepted for any purpose, much less the special fund. The head auditor says that the low-interest loans are beneficial to the Dalenz people and that the payments from the Dalenz government are "just the way they do business."

Chris says she's not convinced and she'd like advice on how to pursue the issue. That night there is a special delivery to Chris's house: all personal items from her office, a letter dismissing her due to "urgent administrative reorganisation" and a cheque for three months' salary as severance pay.

⇒ *Exit 4.* Without telling anyone in the bank, Chris writes an anonymous article in a financial magazine reporting on "financial irregularities" in Dalenz. Although her bank isn't mentioned, there is an immediate investigation to find the source of the story. She is a prime suspect, partly because her denials are half-hearted — lying doesn't come easily. All matters concerning the Dalenz account are removed to higher levels. Chris's job becomes highly unpleasant after a witch hunt for the informant leads to suspicions and petty harassment.

Chris decides to lie low and gather information. Over the next year she collects more information about repression and corruption in Dalenz. She makes copies of documents about payments into and out of the special fund. She makes contact with two independent specialists, one on Dalenz and one on financial institutions and corruption. She prepares a careful account of the Dalenz operation at the bank.

⇒ *Exit 5.* Chris makes a formal submission to the Finance Regulatory Commission, a government body concerned with violation of banking codes. Although submissions are supposed to be confidential, within a matter of days Chris is dismissed. The Commission takes 18 months before ruling that the matters are not in its jurisdiction. Chris sues the bank for improper dismissal under whistleblower legislation, but this fails because she did not use a designated internal channel first. She makes submissions to several other bodies, to no avail. Politicians are similarly unhelpful.

⇒ *Exit 6.* Through an action group FJI, "Financial Justice International," she is put in touch with two other ethical resisters, in different banks, who know about deals with Dalenz. Together they prepare a comprehensive critique that they publish, under pseudonyms, in a magazine specialising on corporate corruption. FJI sends copies to social welfare groups in Dalenz. After resigning and setting up an independent practice, Chris gives her story to the national media. However, only a few alternative newspapers take it up. The bank mounts a concerted attempt to discredit Chris and for several years she barely makes enough to survive on her independent audit consultancy.

⇒ *Exit 7.* A people's movement is emerging in Dalenz, in part stimulated by disgust over high-level government corruption. Chris becomes a valued informant for the movement, providing information and credibility.

Analysis. When corruption reaches to the highest levels — top bank officials, regulatory bodies, politicians — it is extremely difficult to bring about change. From a personal point of view, Chris needed to examine her goals carefully. How important was it to deal with the problem? How important was her own career?

What outsiders can do

Join or set up an action group such as "Financial Justice International." Support people's movements against corruption.

A case of police corruption

Tony was nearly 30 when he joined the police. He had had a number of office jobs and then studied business computing at university, developing an interest in fraud and other white collar crime. After initial police training, he was paired with an old hand, Smithers, dealing with cases of burglary. Tony immediately had to decide how to respond to criminal action by Smithers and others on the burglary squad. Often they would steal from the site of a robbery, taking jewelry, cash and sometimes other goods. Their justification was that "the insurance company pays." If they could find any drugs, they would take and sell them. They considered it a normal benefit of the job — "cream on the cake."

⇒ *Exit 1*. Tony joins in the stealing. He later moves up into the corporate crime section and makes quite a career for himself.

⇒ *Exit 2*. Tony reports the stealing to his commander. He is immediately removed to menial office duties, given a bad report and drummed out of the force.

Tony, through his reading on crime and the police, knew this sort of corruption was commonplace. His toughest task is to not participate while not raising the suspicions of his team-mates, but he manages to pull this off by appearing to sympathise with their actions. He decides to document police theft as much as possible. He keeps a diary of all robbery scenes attended, listing goods taken by Smithers and others. He also makes tapes of some of their conversations, though these were not easy to interpret due to use of police jargon.

Tony planned to lie low and gather as much material as possible. He is horrified to witness several brutal assaults on robbery suspects. He could understand his teammates' frustration. The suspects were almost certainly guilty, yet in many cases there was not enough evidence to convict them, even when the police systematically lied under oath to help the prosecution. Tony tapes some of these incidents of police assault.

⇒ *Exit 3.* After collecting a dossier of damning material, Tony prepares a comprehensive submission to the Police Accountability Agency (PAA), a new body set up to deal with police corruption. After making his submission, Tony is called in by the PAA to discuss what he knows. Shortly afterwards, Tony comes under severe attack. The PAA was supposed to keep his submission confidential, but it becomes clear that some of its members have links to corrupt police. Tony is personally abused by Smithers and others; the tyres to his car are slashed; he finds threatening notes in his locker; his wife and children receive threatening phone calls. The family cat is found killed. In spite of all this, he sticks it out. Then, one day, as he is putting on his jacket, he is arrested. Drugs and a large wad of cash are found in the jacket.

Complaints about him are filed with the PAA. He is dismissed. He thinks about taking the matter to the Ombudsman or a politician but is deterred by the possibility of a criminal charge based on his frame-up.

Tony was aware that the sort of abuse and corruption he was witnessing was tolerated throughout the force. He decides his only hope of success lies with popular outrage generated through media coverage. Police beating of robbery suspects is, unfortunately, not likely to produce all that much concern. But Tony also witnesses some police assaults on innocent individuals, especially homeless people, youths "with an attitude" and racial minorities. One particularly brutal attack results in two young people requiring emergency surgery, and Tony manages to make an audio recording.

⇒ *Exit 4.* Tony takes his documentation to the local media. However, weeks pass and nothing appears. Several journalists tell him it is a good story but that the media cannot afford to run it because the police union has a record for suing, and the costs would be too great. Tony next takes his material to the national media. Television networks are not interested due to lack of a visual dimension — Tony has no videos. Most of the national press do not run the story: it is too much of a local issue to justify the investigative resources required. One crusading magazine, though, runs a major story. Although Tony is not mentioned by name, he is soon identified as the source, and he soon comes under attack, though nothing too blatant, since Tony's team-mates are aware that he might be recording them. After the media attention dies down, he is thoroughly framed — with alteration of official records — put through serious misconduct proceedings and dismissed. The magazine makes a major story of the dismissal, and a few other media outlets take up the issue at this point. However, Tony's career is destroyed.

Tony decides to find allies before going public. As a precaution, he makes multiple copies of all his documentation and gave copies to several trusted friends. He also manages to obtain a copy of his own police file — spotless so far — and makes copies to protect himself in case of future alteration.

After reading further on the problem of police corruption, Tony realises that it is systemic in most police forces and that there is evidence of a national-level "brotherhood." Therefore he cannot expect to address the problem by exposing a few individuals. He makes contact with a national activist group dealing with police abuses and, as a result, meets several police whistleblowers from around the country. He learns from them the incredible personal cost of challenging police corruption from the inside and the virtual impossibility of bringing about change when the major political parties are campaigning on "law and order."

⇒ *Exit 5.* Tony leaves the police and takes another job. He joins a minor political party and works to implement a policy that would address police corruption.

⇒ *Exit 6.* Tony helps the activist group write and produce a booklet designed for people subject to police brutality. The stress of keeping all his outside activity with the group a secret becomes too much and he leaves the force.

⇒ *Exit 7.* Tony decides to keep a low profile and move as soon as he can to the white-collar crime section. Here he finds an outlet for his computer skills. Before long he discovers that corruption pervades this area too. The main differences are that there is no direct violence and the amounts of money are vastly greater. With his links to police whistleblowers he is made constantly aware of the difficulty of exposing problems and building support without sacrificing his career. He keeps collecting information, passing it on to criminology researchers and looking for an avenue to use it where it might actually change things.

Analysis. It is exceedingly risky to expose police corruption from the inside, yet exceedingly difficult to tackle it from the outside. Particular circumstances are required to open the possibility of real change. Tony had a far better chance than most, having prior work experience and skills, yet none of his options guaranteed anything like success.

What outsiders can do

Set up a police corruption action group. Bring together police whistleblowers. Campaign to change policies, such as drug laws, that allow police corruption to flourish.

Lotte Fog blew the whistle on radiation underdosing at Royal Adelaide Hospital. Initially she preferred to be anonymous, hence the silhouette.

A case of sexual harassment

Lydia is a recent engineering graduate who obtains a job in a major corporation. She was one of several female engineers appointed at the same time into an area previously completely dominated by male engineers and technicians. Lydia needs to learn on the job, and some of the technicians know more than anyone about practical things, since many of the senior engineers have managerial roles.

All the female engineers encounter a degree of hostility, especially from the technicians. There is foul language and sexual jokes obviously intended to cause them distress, and they are undermined by not being told about certain standard ways of doing things. One of the other new engineers, Alice, is singled out for harassment: certain men stare at her body while ignoring what she says and put pornographic pictures in her desk drawer. There are incidents where men grab her, ostensibly to protect her from a danger. Alice confides that she is thinking about quitting.

⇒ *Exit 1*. Lydia shows little sympathy. She tries to become "one of the boys," joins in laughter at Alice's expense and ignores the more serious harassment.

⇒ *Exit 2*. Lydia decides to leave at the first opportunity. She thinks she will be the next target after Alice.

⇒ *Exit 3*. Lydia talks to the main harassers, telling them that Alice is seriously upset and thinking of leaving. This only encourages them to escalate their attacks. In a particularly serious incident, Alice suffers a minor injury and then goes on leave for stress. Lydia joins Alice in making a formal complaint to their manager. Nothing happens for months, and the harassment continues. Lydia comes under more systematic attack and eventually leaves. They take the company to court under anti-discrimination legislation. The company fights them tooth and nail, and accuses them of bad performance and even cheating to obtain their engineering qualifications. After two years they lose the case.

Lydia undertakes a systematic study of the problem. She reads books and articles about sexual harassment, and also studies male engineering culture. She talks to sexual harassment counsellors and activists and makes contact with other female engineers who have come up against the problem. She finds out that formal complaints have very little chance of success.

After talking to each of them individually, Lydia calls a meeting of all the female engineers to share their experiences and information. Some of them were not aware of how bad things were for Alice. They agree to support each other. They begin to systematically collect information about every incident of harassment.

⇒ *Exit 4*. After the harassment continues, Lydia and Alice mount a court case under antidiscrimination legislation, thinking that the detailed evidence they've collected will allow them to win against the odds. The case turns their male co-workers against them and, even without overt incidents, the hostility leads both of them to resign. After three tough years they win the case and are awarded compensation. The company appeals. After two more years they settle out of court for a substantial sum, which, however, is small compared to the damage to their careers. Meanwhile, the court case has triggered some superficial changes by management but united the male engineers and technicians against the two women.

⇒ *Exit 5*. The women decide to approach one of the company's new vice-presidents, the first woman to be appointed to this level. The VP tells them they should just tough it out, the same way she did. Later, when contacting female lawyers and counsellors, they find that the VP — an influential person in several circles — has undermined some of their support.

Lydia realises that to change the culture in the workplace, it is necessary to get the support of some male workers. By carefully observing them, she notices that several of them refuse to participate in harassment and a few are obviously repelled by what is happening but are not confident enough to intervene. The women speak to several of these men, emphasising how the harassment is reducing productivity and reducing the chance of making the changes needed to keep the company competitive. They also provide some leaflets on sexual harassment. Two of the men are openly sympathetic. (The wife of one of them is also an engineer, working elsewhere but confronting similar problems.)

Observing a serious "bump-and-grab" incident, one of the sympathetic man speaks critically to the harasser, who in turn becomes very aggressive and nearly starts a fight. A manager happens to witness the entire episode.

⇒ *Exit 6.* The harasser is summarily fired. A trade union official, with strong links to the most serious harassers, gets the technicians to go on strike, telling them that the harasser is the victim of a neurotic feminist who has just broken up with her boyfriend. After the company agrees to abide by the decision of an arbitrator, the technicians return to work. The arbitrator finds that dismissal was too strong an action, and the worker is reinstated. The whole episode mobilises most of the workers behind the harasser, who is seen as a victim of management.

⇒ *Exit 7.* Aware of the increasing tensions, the manager is galvanised into action and is able to implement a "restructuring" that mostly separates the serious harassers from the women. As a result they have an easier time but the culture in the work group with the harassers remains deadly.

Analysis. Sexual harassment is a serious continuing problem, with close links to bullying. If it is deeply entrenched in workplace culture, a long-term strategy oriented to building support is necessary.

What outsiders can do

Join or set up support groups for people who have been sexually harassed. Produce publicity about the problem. Mount campaigns targeting notorious harassers.

Case of an unresponsive anti-corruption agency

Kylie is a middle-ranking manager at a company that successfully tenders for government contracts. She becomes aware of a kick-back scheme by which senior staff at the agency receive payments from companies in exchange for favourable treatment. She wants to expose the scheme but is aware that, if she does so, her own company might lose some of its contracts.

Kylie decides to make an anonymous submission to the Committee on Government Corruption (CGC), an independent government-funded agency set up to investigate and root out corruption in government bodies. Six months after making her detailed submission, nothing has happened. She then rings the CGC and asks what happens with anonymous submissions. She is told that the CGC normally doesn't act on information unless the informants identify themselves, but that identities of all informants are kept in the strictest confidence. With misgivings, Kylie composes and signs a careful letter asking for action on her previous submission.

Soon after, her company loses an expected contract and she is the only person laid off, though her work had been highly regarded. A friendly co-worker tells her that she was suspected of having stabbed the company in the back.

⇒ *Exit 1.* Kylie, severely burned by the experience, moves to another part of the country, obtains another job and vows to stay out of trouble in future.

Months pass, and no action is taken in relation to her submission. Kylie obtains a clerical job and decides to persist with her concerns. She approaches several other agencies but is told that the CGC is the most appropriate body for her complaint. Her calls to the CGC result in bland assurances that her submission is "being looked into."

⇒ *Exit 2.* The CGC is being reviewed after 10 years of operation. Kylie decides to make a complaint to the review committee, pointing out the failure of the CGC to maintain confidentiality. The review committee, however, gives the CGC a favourable report. Talking to a member of the review committee, Kylie is told that there is not any solid evidence that the CGC was responsible for her dismissal.

Kylie, talking to her friends about her problem, is told about someone else who went to the CGC but obtained no satisfaction. She contacts this person, hears a similar story to her own, and is told about others. Soon she has a list of half a dozen people who are disgusted with the CGC, either because it has failed to follow up their information, revealed their identity, or botched investigations so that the main culprits escaped while penalties were imposed on a few scapegoats. Kylie realises that her experiences are typical. She and two others decide to set up the CGC Reform Group.

> ⇒ *Exit 3*. The Reform Group decides to lobby government officials who formally have oversight over the CGC. They muster all their evidence and arguments against the CGC and then prepare submissions and arrange meetings. After two years it is apparent that only superficial changes will be recommended. Most Reform Group members lose interest due to lack of progress.

The Reform Group decides to adopt a strategy based on publicity. After preparing their arguments to be bold and punchy, they contact some journalists and produce media releases accusing the CGC of being "clumsy on corruption." The resulting media stories bring in many new members with further stories of CGC failures. They also stimulate a few individuals to write letters to newspapers in defence of the CGC.

CGC officials do not comment after the first round of stories, obviously hoping the issue will die down. But as the coverage continues week after week — stimulated by new Reform Group members — the CGC issues its own media releases. It also promotes stories about successes in dealing with corruption and attacks the Reform Group for being ignorant and unrepresentative.

⇒ *Exit 4.* The Reform Group maintains its media campaign and is quite successful in denting the image of the CGC. Eventually, though, they run out of fresh stories and journalists and editors lose interest. The CGC weathers the storm and continues on as before, though not as many whistleblowers approach it as before.

Some members of the Reform Group begin a deeper investigation of the CGC, looking into its history, record of performance and also at the record of similar bodies in other countries. They discover that the CGC had never been given the resources or mandate to tackle the most significant forms of corruption — especially corruption linked to the politicians who had set it up — and that it had gradually drifted into a pattern of paper-shuffling (to satisfy stringent bureaucratic reporting requirements), focusing on a few superficial but high-profile cases.

⇒ *Exit 5.* These research-oriented members of the Reform Group prepare several sophisticated papers about the failure of government-initiated campaigns against corruption and get them published in journals and magazines. This academic orientation turns off many other members. In a last-ditch effort to regain momentum, the Reform Group produces an excellent leaflet about the weaknesses of the CGC. However, there is not enough energy to give it wide distribution.

Some members of the Reform Group decide that they need to take action into their own hands. By focussing on the CGC, they were assuming that salvation came from someone else. They decide to set up the "People's Committee on Government Corruption" or PCGC. It would take submissions, establish investigation teams and produce documents. It soon becomes obvious that this is an enormous enterprise and that it will be necessary to concentrate on a few specific areas and types of corruption. PCGC organisers realise that they need to set the highest standards for its investigation teams and that they might be infiltrated or set up. One early spin-off is that two workers at the CGC approach the PCGC with inside information about how the CGC operates and why it has avoided tackling well-known areas of major corruption.

Analysis. Government oversight bodies are often under-resourced and lose any drive to tackle deep-seated problems. Individuals who expect results are often disappointed. Their best chance of changing things comes from banding together. Even then, it is extremely hard to counteract the advantages of a government body with formal legitimacy and connections. Sometimes it can be more productive to take direct action against the problem rather than continuing with a complaint against an official body's lack of action.

What outsiders can do

Join or set up a group such as the CGC Reform Group or the People's Committee on Government Corruption.

11 Surviving

> Whistleblowing can have devastating consequences for health, finances and relationships. You should take steps to maintain each of them.

The personal consequences of whistleblowing or otherwise challenging the system can be severe. Unless you've been through it yourself, it can be worse than you can possibly imagine. There are impacts in three major areas.

Health. The stress of coming under attack can lead to headaches, insomnia, nausea, palpitations, spasms and increased risk of infections, cancer, stroke and heart attack, among others. Psychologically, impacts can include depression, anxiety and paranoia. Many whistleblowers suffer post-traumatic stress disorder.

Finances. Many whistleblowers suffer in their careers, losing out on possible promotions and new jobs. More seriously, they may take a cut in pay or lose their jobs. On top of this, legal and other expenses are often more than $10,000 and sometimes more than $100,000.

Relationships. Getting involved in a major case plays havoc with personal relationships, due to the allegations and rumours, the stress and the time and effort taken fighting the case. This can cause friends and relatives to stay away and can break up marriages.

Impacts in these three areas interact: health and financial problems put a strain on relationships, and a breakdown in relationships can aggravate health problems.

Maintaining good health

The impacts of stress are to some extent unavoidable. If you catch the flu, then it will run its course. But there are ways to reduce the worst consequences.

Regular exercise is important. Walking, aerobics, jogging, swimming and cycling are excellent. They build fitness, reduce bodily tension and have a psychologically calming effect. Some competitive sports can be good too, though there can be tension due to the competition itself.

Good diet is vital. This means eating regularly and in moderation, with plenty of fruit and vegetables. Vitamin-rich and mineral-rich foods are especially important; many people take supplements as well. A wholesome diet makes a big difference in helping resist stress.

This is standard advice, but it can be hard to follow when under intense pressures. There can be a temptation to overeat or to skip meals (depending on the person) and to eat the wrong sorts of foods.

The same applies to drugs. Smoking, alcohol and other drugs may give short-term relief but they can aggravate physical problems and cover up psychological problems.

It can be extremely difficult to change habits, especially in a stressful situation. Willpower is often inadequate. Late at night, after hours spent preparing a submission, it is far more tempting to reach for a smoke or a chocolate than for a carrot stick.

There are several ways to try to overcome this sort of behaviour. One is to ask a family member, friend or co-worker to help. If the rest of the family is eating a wholesome meal, it is easy to join in. If a friend comes by every day to join you for a walk or a swim, it is easier to keep up the habit.

A second way is to design your environment so bad habits are harder to follow. If there are no cigarettes in the house, it's easier to resist the urge for a smoke. If there are tasty fresh fruits always available but no rich cakes, then snacking on the fruit becomes easier.

A third way is to establish a routine to deal with stressful events or times. You might write down a list of "things to do" whenever feeling severely stressed. For example: "(1) take 10 deep, slow breaths; (2) walk around the block; (3) write down exactly what it is that is making me feel stressed; (4) tell myself that I am working hard at making a difference." Pin this list on the wall or put it in your pocket, and then use it. Experiment to find what works for you.

Another important part of maintaining good health is to get plenty of rest. This can be difficult. Insomnia is a common reaction to stress. It is possible to spend half the night awake worrying about what action you should take or what's going to happen next. There are several things that help cope with insomnia. Regular exercise and good diet help. Overuse of cigarettes, alcohol and most other drugs don't. Sleeping pills can help in the short term but over a longer period are undesirable. It is wise to go to bed about the same time every night and, even more importantly, to get up the same time. If you can't sleep, then get up and do something unrelated to what is worrying you, such as read a novel, listen to the radio or do a craft. Lack of sleep on its own is not damaging. If you are sleep-deprived, you can still carry out most tasks with full competence as long as you maintain concentration.

It may seem unfair to have to watch your diet and avoid overindulgence. Why should you? Think of it as being in training. A top swimmer has to put in lots of hours in the pool, eat suitably and get sufficient rest. A whistleblower, in order to succeed against enormous pressures, also needs to put in the required hours of preparation and to make sure their body can withstand the stress. Furthermore, appearing fit and healthy gives you more credibility when meeting others.

Just as important as physical fitness is psychological fitness. This is not just a matter of remaining sane but of keeping a balanced, fresh perspective on the world. This is vital to be able to build support and to formulate and pursue a sensible strategy.

Retaining a sense of perspective in the face of harassment and other pressures is a challenge. If your body is reacting, with insomnia, headaches or worse, this adds to the challenge.

Some pressures are external, and it may not be possible to avoid them. Other pressures are self-imposed, for example spending long hours preparing a submission. Try to moderate the self-imposed pressures. Plan ahead to avoid last-minute demands. Ask for extensions to deadlines. Take regular breaks in work sessions. If you are a perfectionist, ask a friend to help you decide when things are polished enough.

It can help to learn skills in mental relaxation. You could try meditation, learning from a book or a teacher, or something like tai chi, with both physical and mental aspects.

Many people think that emotions just happen and that there is nothing we can do about them. Actually, emotions can be controlled to a considerable extent. You can decide what you want to feel and set about achieving it. Rather than responding to attacks with fear and anger, you can decide that you're going to try to feel filled with confidence, resolve, dignity — even compassion.

One of the ways to do this is through "self-talk." Athletes do this to build their self-confidence and create a deep belief that they can win against the odds. When you are in a secure situation, perhaps just after waking up or before going to sleep, you recite to yourself affirmations such as "I am a worthy person. I will persist with confidence and good humour." If you're a visual person, using appropriate imagery might work better.

What's happening here is that you control your thoughts and this in turn helps shape your emotions. There are limits, though. If a friend of yours dies, it is natural to feel grief. But it is also natural for that grief to decline in intensity over a period of time. If it persists, then it is time to use self-talk to change your emotional state. Similarly, an incident of serious harassment can be expected to lead to strong feelings, such as anger, fear or depression, depending on the person and the circumstances. Through self-talk, these negative emotions can be minimised.

Another approach is meditation in which you simply observe your thoughts without judging them. This process may be enough to make negative thoughts gradually go away. Alternatively, by observing your thoughts, you can identify the ones you want to replace.

Feeling particular emotions can become a habit. After a lifetime of feeling excessive resentment or distress at certain types of situations, it is not easy to change. Don't expect a sudden personality transformation. Just keep working at it.

One way to bring about changes in your emotions is to behave the way you want to feel. For example, you can pretend to be confident even though you feel insecure. If you keep acting confidently for weeks and months, eventually you will start to feel confident.

When under stress, just talking with a sympathetic person can do wonders. It can be a serious mistake to bottle up feelings. The more serious the situation, the more important it is to talk. It can be with a friend or a trained counsellor — someone you trust and who is helpful. If selecting a therapist, try to obtain advice, for example a recommendation from someone who has been in a similar situation. If, for some reason, you are unable to talk about your situation with anyone, you can talk to yourself. Just say out loud what you'd say if someone were there. An alternative is to write it down. A diary can be immensely therapeutic. Speaking and writing help to get things "out of your system."

Surviving financially

A few dissidents don't have to worry about money. They may have large savings or a partner with a secure job. But for the majority, financial survival is a crucial issue. A primary factor that keeps most people from speaking up about problems is fear of loss of income. On top of this, fighting a case through the courts and some other channels can be incredibly expensive.

The keys to surviving financially are to:

- make a complete and honest assessment of one's situation;
- live on a sustainable budget;
- prepare for the worst outcome;
- act now rather than later.

It can be difficult to make a complete and honest assessment of one's finances. Some people don't know what they are spending. Keeping a detailed budget over a month or more can be helpful. Perhaps there are lots of expenses for the mortgage, the car, eating out, medical treatment, buying clothes or sending the children to a private school. The key is to be aware of them.

Once you know your financial situation, work out a budget that you can maintain, so less money is going out than is coming in. Ideally you should be saving some money too.

Next, prepare for the worst outcome. If you are being seriously threatened with dismissal, then prepare for dismissal and a period without work. If you are pursuing a legal case, it may take twice as long as the lawyer predicts and cost twice as much. If you win, the other side may appeal. The worst case is that you lose. Take this into account when, for example, considering whether to ask to borrow money from relatives.

If you lose your job, you need to cut expenses immediately. It's tempting to keep up the same lifestyle in the hope that you'll get your job back in an appeal or find a new one. This is risky and can make things far worse later on. It may be wise to move to cheaper lodging, sell or do without certain luxury items, or to change to less expensive habits or hobbies.

Cutting expenses may seem like giving up. Indeed, in a few situations, maintaining appearances can be important to winning a case. But usually the cost of your clothes and the newness of your car are far less important than your ability to survive and keep fighting the case. You are much more likely to survive if you are living within your finances and prepared for the worst outcome. Otherwise, due to lack of money, you may have to give up in the middle of the struggle.

If you win a big settlement or get your job back, it's time to celebrate. But don't assume money problems are over. If you can't get a job or are dismissed again, your bank balance could dwindle to nothing before you know it. Prudent financial planning is essential to give you long-term security.

Maintaining relationships

Pursuing a case can become an all-consuming struggle, taking up every waking minute and every thought. Since you're struggling for your beliefs and your life, it's natural to become single-minded. Since you talk only about your case, your relatives, friends and co-workers will start to think you're obsessed. They're right!

There are two important reasons why maintaining relationships should be a priority. First, personal relationships are important in themselves. For most people, they are an essential part of a life worth living. Is your case so very important that it's worth alienating those closest to you?

Struggles are often far more intense and long-lasting than ever imagined at the beginning. A friend who starts off making a temporary sacrifice may eventually find it becomes too much. Rekindling friendships may not be so easy. Of course, the struggle may help you decide who your "real" friends are. But do you want the struggle to define all your relationships?

The second important reason why maintaining relationships should be a priority is that it can help you succeed in your struggle. Your family, friends and co-workers are potential allies. They can give you practical assistance and emotional support. It's far better to win them over than turn them off.

Your case may be the most important thing in your life but it won't be for most other people. A few may share your passion but many others will prefer you to be the way you used to be.

Spend time with those you care about the most. If you are spending lots of time on a case, you won't be able to do all the socialising you used to do. Time with those closest to you should be a priority.

Focus on the other person. Listen to their concerns and perspectives. If the other person has heard a lot from you about the case, one useful technique is not to raise it unless they ask. Then, be brief and let them ask for more information if they want to. For casual acquaintances, use only the briefest of summaries. If they want to know more, let them ask. If you have a write-up, that can replace a lengthy repeat of the story.

There are several advantages to saying less rather than more. You are better able to maintain relationships and avoid alienating people. You create a better image as a sensible, balanced person, and this can help you succeed in the struggle. You can get a better sense of how other people perceive and react if you listen rather than talk. Understanding other people's perspectives is very helpful in making your own message more effective and keeping your case in context.

12 Whistleblower groups

> A whistleblower group can both support individuals and help tackle social problems. Options include networks, support groups and action groups.

One of the most useful things for any person with a special problem is to talk with others who have similar experiences. This is true of men with prostate cancer, children of alcoholics — and whistleblowers. When whistleblowers meet each other, it can be remarkably beneficial. For some, it is the first time they have talked with anyone who really understands what they've been going through. The relief and reassurance this provides to someone who has been under constant attack is hard to appreciate.

So, just contact some local whistleblowers, call a meeting and away you go! That can be all it takes. But things are seldom this simple.

Here I will outline some factors to consider in organising to support whistleblowers. This draws heavily on my experience with Whistleblowers Australia but includes insights from other groups.

Getting started

In a city of 100,000 people, there are probably dozens of people with whistleblowing experience and many with current cases. As well, there will be others who are sympathetic or concerned, such as free speech campaigners. Finding out who these people are may not be so easy. One way is to ask prominent whistleblowers, whether local or from elsewhere. Individuals whose stories are in the media are often contacted by others with similar experiences. Another way is to search the Internet or news databases. Over a year, it wouldn't be surprising if several cases were reported. Finally, there is publicity. An advertisement or, far better, an article or news story about whistleblowing is an excellent way to encourage people to contact you.

Sometimes, though, there are plenty of people known to be willing to attend a meeting, but no one is willing to do the work. Calling a meeting is not a big operation. Find a venue — a person's home, or a room in a library, church or school — select a date and time, and send out notices. But someone has to do the organising, and only a minority of people will take the initiative and associated responsibility. Action groups and support groups depend on these organisers. Many groups never start because there is no such person. Others depend on one person, without whom the group would collapse. For a group to have resilience, there should be several people who will take responsibility. That's the best situation.

From now on, I'm assuming that there is at least one organiser. The next question is, what should be done? There are a number of possibilities, each with advantages and disadvantages.

Networks

A network is essentially a set of actual or potential links between people. It could be a list, with each person providing contact information, their areas of knowledge and experience, and what they are potentially willing to do to help dissidents, such as provide advice, write letters or talk to the media. After that, it all depends on someone's initiative. A journalist can use the list to find people willing to speak on particular topics. Someone on the list might send articles to everyone else on the list. Many networks operate through email lists, Facebook pages, Googlegroups or other platforms.

When you think about it, it's obvious that every organisation has one or more associated networks. Employees know each other, or at least some of them know each other. They may just meet on the job, or they may ring each other at home, go to parties, etc. The same applies to church members, club members and students, among others.

In all these cases, there is an organisation and a network. A pure network, in contrast, doesn't have an organisation. There are no meetings, no money, no constitution, no office bearers. There's just the list or online venue, and everything else is at someone's initiative. The key exception is that one or two people need to take responsibility for maintaining the network. As in most voluntary activities, organisers are vital.

Many contacts occur through personal referral. When someone asks me for advice, I often suggest that they contact certain other people. Other contacts arise when people search the web and find an article or blog or whatever — and a link to you. If you are mentioned in a newspaper or give a talk on radio, people with similar concerns may be inspired to contact you.

A network is more than a list of names or a website. It is a process, a set of active relationships. If a network is active, it usually means that its members are engaged with the issues as well as with each other.

People involved in groups often begin to think that the organisational aspects — meetings, regulations, policies — are central, and forget about the network aspects. In reality, networks are crucial features of organisations, and sometimes more important than the organisation itself.

Individual support

If someone rings with a problem, you may be able to offer information, support and advice. Individual support is one of the most vital parts of helping whistleblowers and promoting dissent. It doesn't require great knowledge, but rather a sensitivity to a person and their concerns. There are a few things that are often helpful.

1. Listening. Often a person with a problem just needs someone to listen without judging them. They may be able to work out a solution themselves without any advice. There can be a great temptation to jump in and tell a person what they should be doing. That may be counterproductive. People need to reach their own decisions. What can help, sometimes, is suggestions of options or implications — but not a long lecture. Listen ... listen.

2. Contacts. You may be able to suggest people who can help or who have had similar experiences. Maybe there is an organisation or a meeting. A lot of support is helping a person make the right contacts. (Back to the networks.)

3. Information. You may have articles or other materials that can help. (See below.)

Nearly everyone has much to offer in giving individual support, if they want to. If you want to improve your listening skills, observe others who are good at this, for example at meetings. Ask for feedback from people you talk to. Try some role plays in "active listening." For improving knowledge of contacts, talk to people yourself, ask people for their recommendations, attend meetings and get advice from good networkers. For improving knowledge of information sources, read things yourself and ask others what was most helpful to them.

Information materials

Talking to people is fine but it takes time and can become repetitive. Giving someone an article or link that addresses their particular situation can be extremely helpful. To provide support effectively, it's valuable to have a collection of materials, so the most relevant ones can be given to a person seeking assistance.

Short treatments are often most helpful to begin with. Short articles are good and so are copies of news stories. Books and lengthy reports can be helpful for those who have a deeper interest.

What should the materials be about?

- Information about the topic, whether it is ethics in the workplace, corruption, what happens to whistleblowers, or methods of responding.
- Contacts: names, addresses, phone numbers.
- Where to get more information: organisations, websites, links to articles and books.

For some people, a packet of information materials is the main help they'll receive. They may be isolated geographically or socially, or they may be in a risky position and nervous about speaking too widely about their case. Information kits should be designed and chosen to help people to become as self-reliant as possible.

Support groups and action groups

Whistleblowers can form support groups or action groups — both of which are described in chapter 9 — or groups that are combinations of both. Support groups probably offer the best chance of giving whistleblowers more confidence and support without the distraction of formal procedures and business. They aren't necessarily easy to run, and sometimes they are filled with tension and anguish — many whistleblowers need a lot of support — but it's worth the effort.

Whistleblower action groups can use a variety of methods, including lobbying politicians, producing newsletters and reports, carrying out investigations, making informed public statements, writing letters, organising meetings and promoting civil disobedience. They can have various goals, such as promoting whistleblower legislation, changing laws or policies that constrain free speech of employees, opposing the use of defamation law against free speech, exposing corruption and injustice in specific areas (police, banks, building industry, etc.), opposing censorship or promoting open government. Here I'll just give a few brief comments about some key issues facing whistleblower and related groups.

Action versus support. In many groups there is a mixture of functions, including both action and support. Getting the balance right is hard. Some people are coming to get things done — action. They are oriented to tasks. Others are seeking support. They are primarily concerned about maintaining relationships.

Support or maintenance is always involved, at some level. If support functions are neglected, personal tensions can tear a group apart. On the other hand, if support becomes the primary focus, nothing gets done. Sometimes it can help to separate these functions, for example to having personal sharing at the beginning of a meeting, or by having separate support and general business meetings.

Advocacy. Should the group take up an individual member's personal case, and thus become involved in advocacy? Or should it stick to support, education, publicity, lobbying and/or direct action?

Some individual cases are very worthy. Such cases can provide leverage for wider change, and associated publicity can further the cause. The disadvantage is that advocacy is inevitably selective. Due to shortage of resources, only some cases can be supported. That means not supporting others. If people expect to find advocates, most will be disappointed. If they expect to obtain a sympathetic ear, some information and a few contacts, there's a better chance of meeting their expectations.

Openness. Should the group be open to all comers? Or should it be restricted to those who satisfy certain criteria?

If a whistleblower group is restricted to those who are "genuine" whistleblowers, what is to be done about someone who has spent time in prison and claims he was framed because he spoke out? Someone has to judge each claim, and this can be contentious. Some who aren't whistleblowers will slip through the net and some who are genuine may be put off by the process of scrutiny. On the other hand, all sorts of people can attend an open group, and this may include a few disruptive ones who are given no credence by anyone else.

Jean Lennane comments

Whistleblowers are normally very conscientious and often somewhat obsessional people, who by definition won't shut up and go away. When they first come to a whistleblower group, they are also almost always totally preoccupied with the importance and injustice of their own case. This can make it difficult to run a group. Be aware and be prepared!

Becoming able to step back from one's own case to see the bigger picture is vital in the healing process and makes people far more effective in tackling the system. Once there is a core of whistleblowers who have reached this stage, a group becomes much more productive as well as far easier to run.

Hierarchy. The traditional bureaucratic model is based on hierarchy. People in positions at the top have the most power and issue orders to subordinates. Voluntary groups like churches also can operate bureaucratically, even though those at the top have little or no legal authority. An alternative model is of equality, in which all members are equal in formal status, with no office bearers. Often in such groups there is an attempt to rotate tasks and develop each person's skills in different areas.

The hierarchical model gives some advantages. Official office bearers have more status and credibility with the media. If, as is usual, they have lots of experience and skill, their positions give them official sanction to make key decisions and set policy. But there are disadvantages. Hierarchy tends to breed power struggles. Ambitious or status-conscious people seek positions at the top not because of what they have to offer but because they want power and status. Others become resentful. This can result in spiteful battles, including cliques, backstabbing, sabotage and alienation of members.

Without official leaders, egalitarian groups sometimes have a difficult time gaining a media profile. On the other hand, they are often more satisfying for members. However, power struggles can occur even when there are no formal positions of authority. In all groups there are differences in experience, knowledge, skills and relationships. Some people use these to obtain advantages or personal rewards for themselves, such as recognition or paid travel, and others may be resentful of those with talent. There can be some standard problems, such as hoarding of information, rumours, formation of factions, and attempts to gain power or undermine others, that are common in virtually all groups. Hierarchical groups, though, tend to have these to a greater degree. There are a number of ways to minimise concentration of power in traditional organisations, including limited terms for office bearers, postal ballots, external mediators and random selection of chairs for meetings.

> Whistleblowers Australia, most of whose members are whistleblowers, has provided personal support and advice to hundreds of individuals, produced a variety of information materials and waged campaigns on several important topics (such as the right of workers to make public interest disclosures without reprisal). This activity has been an important factor in creating a wider awareness in the media and the community of the significance of whistleblowing. Although Whistleblowers Australia has had its share of internal strife, its experience shows that whistleblower groups can make a difference.

Assessment

There's no single best way to promote the cause of whistleblowing. Networks, individual support, information materials, support groups and action groups can all be valuable. Each person can contribute in their own way, for example by offering support to a friend, joining an action group or writing a letter or submission. Different approaches are needed, because no single approach is right for everyone and every circumstance. We need to help others find the best way they can contribute, and to keep learning about how to improve. The task is large but, as long as people care, there is hope.

References

For those who want information, the most common approach is to put "whistleblowing" into a search engine and see what comes up. If you get to any of the major sites hosted by whistleblower-support organisations — such as the Government Accountability Project — they will offer much valuable information as well as links to other sites and sources.

There are numerous books about whistleblowing, plus many personal accounts by whistleblowers, as well as films such as *The Insider* and *The Whistleblower*. Most of these are informative. Despite different circumstances, the experiences of whistleblowers frequently follow a standard pattern, so learning about what happens to others can provide helpful lessons.

In this context of an abundance of information, I offer here only a few references, with an emphasis on the areas I've covered. My own website is http://www.bmartin.cc/dissent/, with many documents, contacts and links to other sites — including links to several of the articles cited here.

Practical guides

Tom Devine, *The Whistleblower's Survival Guide: Courage Without Martyrdom* (Washington, DC: Fund for Constitutional Government, 1997), available at http://www.whistleblower.org/program-areas/gap-reports/. Many whistleblowers have said this is the most practical manual available. It has lots of information about US official channels which, however, is of limited value to people elsewhere.

Tom Devine and Tarek F. Maassarani, *The Corporate Whistleblower's Survival Guide* (San Francisco: Berrett-Koehler, 2011). An up-to-date comprehensive treatment, highly valuable. Much of the information is geared to US circumstances.

Jean Lennane, "What happens to whistleblowers, and why," in Klaas Woldring (ed.), *Business Ethics in Australia and New Zealand: Essays and Cases* (Melbourne: Thomas Nelson, 1996), pp. 51–63. A valuable summary of insights. Reprinted in 2012 in the online journal *Social Medicine*.

Books about whistleblowing

C. Fred Alford, *Whistleblowers: Broken Lives and Organizational Failure* (Ithaca, NY: Cornell University Press, 2001). A thought-provoking assessment of the meaning of the whistleblower experience, with a penetrating analysis of how whistleblowers' lives and beliefs are destroyed.

Richard Calland and Guy Dehn (editors), *Whistleblowing around the World: Law, Culture and Practice* (Cape Town: Open Democracy Advice Centre; London: Public Concern at Work, 2004). An excellent collection of case studies, assessments of legal protection, and civil society responses.

William De Maria, *Deadly Disclosures: Whistleblowing and the Ethical Meltdown of Australia* (Adelaide: Wakefield Press, 1999). Many detailed case studies, with a pessimistic view about prospects.

Myron Peretz Glazer and Penina Migdal Glazer, *The Whistleblowers: Exposing Corruption in Government and Industry* (New York: Basic Books, 1989). A vivid picture of whistleblowers' commitment and courage and the terrible reprisals visited on them.

Geoffrey Hunt (ed.), *Whistleblowing in the Health Service: Accountability, Law and Professional Practice* (London: Edward Arnold, 1995).

Geoffrey Hunt (ed.), *Whistleblowing in the Social Services: Public Accountability and Professional Practice* (London: Arnold, 1998).

Roberta Ann Johnson, *Whistleblowing: When It Works — and Why* (Boulder, CO: Lynne Rienner, 2003). Treatment of relatively successful high-profile US cases.

Marcia P. Miceli, Janet P. Near and Terry Morehead Dworkin, *Whistle-blowing in Organizations* (New York: Routledge, 2008). A comprehensive review of research.

Terance D. Miethe, *Whistleblowing at Work: Tough Choices in Exposing Fraud, Waste, and Abuse on the Job* (Boulder, CO: Westview, 1999). An informative, logical, balanced survey of whistleblowing in the US.

Bureaucracy

Mark Bovens, *The Quest for Responsibility: Accountability and Citizenship in Complex Organisations* (Cambridge: Cambridge University Press, 1998). A political, ethical and organisational design analysis of how to control complex organisations by using demands for accountability.

Deena Weinstein, *Bureaucratic Opposition: Challenging Abuses at the Workplace* (New York: Pergamon, 1979). A valuable perspective for understanding the nature of bureaucracy as a power system and the implications for whistleblowers.

The psychology of wrongdoing

People who do bad things seldom think of themselves as bad people. These books give an insight into what's really going through people's minds.

Roy F. Baumeister, *Evil: Inside Human Violence and Cruelty* (New York: Freeman, 1997).

Fred Emil Katz, *Ordinary People and Extraordinary Evil: A Report on the Beguilings of Evil* (Albany, NY: State University of New York Press, 1993).

Low-profile operations — and surviving in organisations

There is no definitive treatment of how to bring about bottom-up change within organisations. These books deal with survival or fostering change or both.

Lee G. Bolman and Terrence E. Deal, *Escape from Cluelessness: A Guide for the Organizationally Challenged* (New York: Amacom, 2000). Advice for understanding and promoting change in US corporations.

Ira Chaleff, *The Courageous Follower: Standing up to and for our Leaders* (San Francisco: Berrett-Koehler, 2003). How to help the organisation by serving when appropriate and gently challenging leaders as needed.

Harry E. Chambers, *My Way or the Highway: The Micromanagement Survival Guide* (San Francisco: Berrett-Koehler, 2004). On dealing with controlling managers.

Laura Crawshaw, *Taming the Abrasive Manager: How to End Unnecessary Roughness in the Workplace* (San Francisco: Jossey-Bass, 2007). On what drives overbearing bosses and how to deal with them.

Leonard Felder, *Fitting in Is Overrated: The Survival Guide for Anyone Who Has Ever Felt Like an Outsider* (New York: Sterling, 2009). The benefits of and skills for being different.

Joep P. M. Schrijvers, *The Way of the Rat: A Survival Guide to Office Politics* (London: Cyan, 2004). A practical manual, presented from a cynical perspective.

Judith Wyatt and Chauncey Hare, *Work Abuse: How to Recognize and Survive It* (Rochester, VT: Schenkman, 1997). A comprehensive treatment on surviving psychologically, well worth detailed study.

Verbal skills

Verbal skills can make a tremendous difference in bringing about change.

Suzette Haden Elgin, *The Gentle Art of Verbal Self-Defense* (New York: Fall River, 2009, revised edition) — and many other books with related titles. A highly insightful, practical treatment.

Sam Horn, *Tongue Fu! How to Deflect, Disarm, and Defuse any Verbal Conflict* (New York: St. Martin's Griffin, 1996). A wonderful manual on effective verbal communication.

George J. Thompson and Jerry B. Jenkins, *Verbal Judo: The Gentle Art of Persuasion* (New York: William Morrow, 1993). An excellent practical treatment on how to be effective verbally.

Official channels

There is no single reference that gives a comprehensive description of how and why official channels fail so often. These treatments deal with aspects of the problem.

William De Maria and Cyrelle Jan, "Behold the shut-eyed sentry! Whistleblower perspectives on government failure to correct wrongdoing," *Crime, Law & Social Change*, Vol. 24, 1996, pp. 151–166.

Thomas M. Devine and Donald G. Aplin, "Abuse of authority: the Office of the Special Counsel and whistleblower protection," *Antioch Law Journal*, Vol. 4, No. 5, 1986, pp. 5–71.

Thomas M. Devine and Donald G. Aplin, "Whistleblower protection–the gap between the law and reality," *Howard Law Journal*, Vol. 31, 1988, pages 223–239.

Anthony J. Evans, "Dealing with dissent: whistleblowing, egalitarianism, and the republic of the firm," *Innovation: the European Journal of Social Science Research*, Vol. 21, No. 3, September 2008, pp. 267–279.

Thane Rosenbaum, *The Myth of Moral Justice: Why Our Legal System Fails to Do What's Right* (New York: HarperCollins, 2004).

Leaking

The Art of Anonymous Activism: Serving the Public While Surviving Public Service (Washington, DC: Project on Government Oversight; Government Accountability Project; Public Employees for Environmental Responsibility, 2002), especially pp. 7–16. A practical manual, oriented to US circumstances.

Julian Assange, "How a whistleblower should leak information." (Search for it on the web.) Very sensible advice.

Kathryn Flynn, "The practice and politics of leaking," *Social Alternatives*, Vol. 30, No. 1, 2011, pp. 24–28. A nice summary treatment.

Nicky Hager and Bob Burton, *Secrets and Lies: The Anatomy of an Anti-environmental PR Campaign* (Nelson, New Zealand: Craig Potton, 1999). An appendix, "A brief guide to leaking," is informative.

Strategy for activists

For skills on analysing the situation, developing a strategy and taking action, see:

Saul Alinsky, *Rules for Radicals: a Practical Primer for Realistic Radicals* (New York: Random House, 1971).

Doyle Canning and Patrick Reinsborough, *Re:imagining Change: An Introduction to Story-based Strategy* (smartMeme, 2009).

Virginia Coover, Ellen Deacon, Charles Esser and Christopher Moore, *Resource Manual for a Living Revolution* (Philadelphia: New Society Publishers, 1981).

Chris Crass, *Towards Collective Liberation: Anti-Racist Organizing, Feminist Praxis, and Movement Building Strategy* (Oakland, CA: PM Press, 2013).

Per Herngren, *Path of Resistance: The Practice of Civil Disobedience* (Philadelphia: New Society Publishers, 1993).

Brian Martin, *Backfire Manual: Tactics against Injustice* (Sparsnäs, Sweden: Irene Publishing, 2012). How to make attacks counterproductive for the attacker.

Bill Moyer, with JoAnn McAllister, Mary Lou Finley, and Steven Soifer, *Doing Democracy: The MAP Model for Organizing Social Movements* (Gabriola Island, BC, Canada: New Society Publishers, 2001).

Randy Shaw, *The Activist's Handbook: A Primer for the 1990s and Beyond* (Berkeley: University of California Press, 2001).

Katrina Shields, *In the Tiger's Mouth: An Empowerment Guide for Social Action* (Sydney: Millennium Books, 1991).

War Resisters' International, *Handbook for Nonviolent Campaigns* (War Resisters' International, 2009).

Surviving

There is a lot of writing about "resilience," at work and elsewhere. Use this as a keyword to find recent sources.

Roy F. Baumeister and John Tierney, *Willpower: Rediscovering Our Greatest Strength* (Penguin, 2011). On understanding and using willpower.

Salvatore R. Maddi and Deborah M. Khoshaba, *Resilience at Work: How to Succeed No Matter What Life Throws at You* (New York: Amacom, 2005).

James W. Pennebaker, *Opening Up: The Healing Power of Expressing Emotions* (New York, Guilford, 1997). Writing as a tool for dealing with emotional problems. This is one of several works by Pennebaker helpful to anyone under stress.

Kathryn D. Cramer, *Staying on Top When Your World Turns Upside Down* (New York: Penguin, 1990).

Index

action groups, 137–138, 171–173, 202, 214–215, 219, 244–248, 255–256. *See also* direct action; social action
advice, 53–55, 75–80, 116, 120–124, 167
advocates, 120–124, 145–146. *See also* lawyers
analysis, 60–61
anonymity. *See* leaking; secrecy
attack: methods of, 31–37; reasons for, 37–38

behaviour, 144–145
blacklisting, 34
blaming, 27–28
bullying, 24, 207–211, 224. *See also* harassment
bureaucracy, 44–49, 251–252.

complaints, 41–42. *See also* official channels
computers, 143–144
contacts, 243
context, 70–73
corporations, 44–49

corruption: financial, 211–215; police, 215–219. *See also* problems
Cosser, Robina, 7, 33, 35, 53, 55, 108, 179
cover-up, 36–37. *See also* secrecy
co-workers, 32, 77–78, 85, 87. *See also* support

De Maria, Bill, 93–94, 251
defamation, 162, 186, 189
devaluation, 36–37. *See also* rumours
dialogue, 42–43, 52–53, 168. *See also* person-to-person approaches
diaries, 67. *See also* written account
direct action, 156–158. *See also* action groups; social action
disability, 159–161
dobbing, 50
doctors, 18, 30, 61–62, 79–80. *See also* health
documents, 65–70, 142. *See also* evidence
double standard test, 39–40

Ellsberg, Daniel, 131

emotions, 14, 115, 120. *See also* motives
evidence, 11, 13, 53–55, 65–70

family, 19, 76, 146–148, 231, 236. *See also* support
financial survival, 234–236
Fog, Lotte, 220
formal channels. See official channels
friends, 19, 76–77, 119–120, 146, 166, 231, 236. *See also* support

goals, 57–63
government, 90–91, 100–102. *See also* official channels

harassment, 24, 32–33, 95; sexual, 70, 220–224. *See also* bullying
health, 230–234. *See also* doctors; emotions
hierarchy, 247–248. *See also* powerholders
hotlines, 149–150

information, 243–244. *See also* documents; evidence; references; research
intimidation, 36–37. *See also* reprisals

Jackall, Robert, 44–49
journalists, 15, 135–137, 139–140, 146, 158, 181–188, 191. *See also* media

Kardell, Cynthia, 7, 27, 56, 59, 62, 66, 79, 80, 104, 105, 110, 120, 123, 125, 132–133, 140

language, 50, 195

lawyers, 79–80, 109–110, 121, 122, 125, 146, 183. *See also* advocates
leaking, 6, 50, 129–150, 254–255
Lennane, Jean, 7, 69, 71, 93, 122, 159, 246, 250
letters, 14, 66, 100–102, 173–177, 183–184
Lindeberg, Kevin, 63, 204
listening, 243
low-profile operations, 81–88, 252–253. *See also* verbal skills

MacGregor, Isla, 7, 78
media, mass, 180–191. *See also* journalists
mediation, 125–128
Moral Mazes, 44–49
motives, 55–57, 112. *See also* emotions

networks, 241–243
newspapers, 187, 190. *See also* journalists; media
news values, 181–182

official channels, 5, 36–37, 89–128, 149–150, 154–155, 157–158, 180, 182–183, 254; choosing, 102–118; failure of, 91–99
opponents, 166–168
opportunity cost, 62–63, 113
ostracism, 32, 34

person-to-person approaches, 165–168
photos, 67
Pinson, Lesley, 7, 73, 79–80, 94, 96, 112, 121–122, 154, 190–191
police, 21, 30, 135, 215–219
power, 40–41. *See also* powerholders

powerholders, 36–37, 74, 152–157, 182–183
preparation, 65–80
pressure group politics, 155–157. See also action groups
problems, 23–28, 39–43
psychology of wrongdoing, 252

radio, 187, 190. See also media
recordings, 67, 69–70, 164–165
references, 249–256. See also information
relationships, 236–237. See also co-workers; family; friends
reprisals, 31–37
research, 72–73, 109–110, 118–120. See also information; scientific fraud
rumours, 31–33, 82–83

sabotage, 192–195
scientific fraud, 202–207
secrecy, 36–37, 194. See also leaking; low-profile operations
self-respect, 76, 112
Serpico, Frank, 21
sexual harassment, 220–224
silencing clauses, 124–125
Silkwood, Karen, 175
social action, 50, 255–256. See also action groups; direct action
solutions, 27, 74–75
speaking, 119–120. See also verbal skills
statements, 67–68
strategy, 59–63, 81, 124, 191–192, 255–256
style, 13–14, 144, 176–177
success, 115–118

support: building, 15–16, 151–195; getting, 75–80; groups, 168–171, 244–248; individual, 242–243
surviving, 229–237, 256
sympathisers, 166–168. See also relationships; support

threats, 32–34
timing, 14–15, 38
traps, 9–20
trust, 9–11, 18, 54, 109–110, 136
TV, 190–191. See also media

unions, 77–80

verbal skills, 253

websites, 177–180
whistleblower groups, 239–249. See also action groups; support groups
Whistleblowers Australia, 5, 33, 71, 93, 105, 239, 241, 248
whistleblowing: attackers' perception of, 43–49; consequences of, 29–37, 229–230; language of, 50; references, 250–251; traps in, 9–20
Wigand, Jeffrey, 17
WikiLeaks, 139–140
workplace injury, 198–202
written account, 158–165

Printed in Great Britain
by Amazon.co.uk, Ltd.,
Marston Gate.